Brookshire & Belk

Brookshire & Belk

BUSINESSMEN
IN CITY HALL

By
Alex Coffin

The University of North Carolina at Charlotte,

Charlotte, North Carolina 28223

© 1994 by The University of North Carolina at Charlotte

All rights reserved. Published 1994

Printed in the United States of America

by Monarch Printing, Inc.

Charlotte, North Carolina

Library of Congress Cataloging-in-Publication Data

Coffin, Alex, 1936–

    Brookshire & Belk, businessmen in city hall / by Alex Coffin.

        p.   cm.

    Includes index.

    ISBN 0-945344-01-5 : $19.95

    1. Charlotte (N.C.)—Politics and government. 2. Brookshire, Stanford R., 1905- . 3. Belk, John M., 1921- . I. Title. II. Title: Brookshire and Belk, businessmen in city hall.

F264.C4C64 1994

975.6 ' 76—dc20   94-27729

                                 CIP

This book is dedicated to my parents, Parinne "Penny" Smith Coffin and the late Harris A. Coffin, and to my late great-uncle, Oscar Jackson "Skipper" Coffin, former dean of the University of North Carolina School of Journalism.

Contents

Acknowledgements / ix

Preface / xiii

Introducing the Era / 1

**Part One
Stan Brookshire 1961–1969**

What Was Happening Elsewhere / 5

Chapter One
"No, Not Interested!" / 7
Chapter Two
The People and How They Got Along / 21
Chapter Three
How Segregated Was Charlotte? / 41
Chapter Four
Rebuilding the Downtown Area / 71
Chapter Five
Roads—Where They Were Built and Why / 87
Chapter Six
**What Charlotte Had Was Really a Small-Town
        Airport / 97**
Chapter Seven
**Planning, Reports, and Related Items—What Worked
        and What Didn't / 103**
Chapter Eight
A Grab Bag—Bond Issues and Blue Laws / 109

Part Two
John Belk 1969–1977

What Was Happening Elsewhere / 123

Chapter Nine
The Millionaire Bachelor / 125
Chapter Ten
The People and How They Got Along . . . or Didn't / 143
Chapter Eleven
Race Relations—Things Continue to Improve / 171
Chapter Twelve
**The Downtown Is Transformed . . . and Becomes the
    Uptown / 183**
Chapter Thirteen
Roads—A Never-Ending Problem / 205
Chapter Fourteen
Airport Development—Entering the Big Time / 211
Chapter Fifteen
Planning and Parks and Related Things / 219
Chapter Sixteen
**Making City Hall Businesslike . . . Strikes . . . and Secrecy
    / 225**
Drawing Some Conclusions / 249
Closing Out the Era / 251

City Government Officials During the Brookshire and Belk
    Eras / 255
Index / 261
Photography Credits / 273

Acknowledgements

I am indebted to many people for their emotional and practical support during the writing of this book. Perhaps most of all I am grateful to the scores of people who gave up their valuable time to chat with me and let me tap their memories of times long gone by. I was touched by how helpful and gracious everyone was. It was wonderful to renew some old friendships. Tops among this group were Bill Veeder and John Morrisey. I need to add that Veeder lost his crusty reputation after he prepared an elaborate lunch when I visited him on his farm near Henderson. And Bill Carstarphen, former assistant city manager under Brookshire and Belk and city manager in Greensboro in 1994, took several hours from his busy schedule and helped me considerably. I also would like to single out the direct and indirect contributions of writer Neal Peirce, who graciously remembered that I took him on a tour of Atlanta in February 1969 for a book he was doing and who gave me my first mention in a book. I am extremely grateful to Sara Klemmer and her staff at *The Charlotte Observer* library for putting up with me and all my unusual requests over more than six months. Among others who deserve special credit are my wife Sonia Kulka Coffin and friend Randy Whitt, who read the manuscript and found mistakes I missed; supportive friends Erskine Harkey and Bill Yoder; graphic designer Barbara Howard and photographer Donna Bise, two thoroughly outstanding professionals; as well as David Burkhalter, Ray Killian and Darrell Williams of Belk Stores; Stan Brookshire Jr. and Carolyn Sachsenmaier, the late mayor's son and daughter; Karen Sachsenmaier, his granddaughter; Robin Brabham and Randy Penninger of the UNC Charlotte Library; *Charlotte Observer* reporter Lew Powell, who provided his former colleague Susan Jetton's notes from 1976 on John Belk's humorous quotes; M.S. Van Hecke, former *Charlotte Observer* business editor; Jenny Rosenthal at the Charlotte-Mecklenburg Public Library; Jane Miles and Cheryl Ramsaur Roberts at the UNC Charlotte Urban Institute; Schley Lyons, UNC Charlotte political scientist; Reid Washam, Brenda Freeze and Belinda Crowell at City Hall; Janet Warren at the Charlotte Chamber; Rich Oppel, former *Charlotte Observer* editor; and my office landlord and friend of nine years, Robert Morrison. If I misinterpreted someone's remarks, or misquoted them, I hope they will forgive me. I promise it wasn't intentional.

I covered Charlotte's schools in 1962–63 and city government in 1964–65 and did stories on the 1969 Charlotte city election for *The Atlanta Constitution*. Although I can't claim to have been close personal friends with either Stan Brookshire or John Belk, I was acquainted with each over a period of about 30 years.

I purposely repeated identifications of those mentioned several times in the book to keep readers from having to flip back and forth to determine who's who.

I have tried to be true to the times in using terms that were used by a majority of people at the time. For example, the correct term was then Negro, later black and now

African-American. It was then the Civic Center, now the Convention Center. It was then the Charlottetown Mall, it is now the Midtown Square. It was then downtown, it is now uptown. It was then NCNB, it is now NationsBank. It was then Betty Chafin and Pat Locke, it is now Betty Chafin Rash and Pat Locke Williamson. And there are numerous other examples. Admittedly, I may have missed a few so I ask your tolerance. I tried to avoid insulting any group, minority or otherwise, but my biases might show through despite my efforts.

Preface

This book, commissioned by the University of North Carolina at Charlotte, chronicles the events that took place within city government in Charlotte, North Carolina, over nearly a two-decade period. The book is divided into two parts, covering Stan Brookshire's eight years and then John Belk's eight years in City Hall. Each part covers issues and events that were identified as particularly interesting and significant during those time periods. Because the beginning and the end of some historical events bridged the Brookshire and Belk eras, they are discussed in both parts. The specific period—1961 to 1977—was chosen because from the advantage of the passing of time in 1994 it seemed that era exemplified a unique relationship between the business community and the political leadership of the city. Further, it seemed to be a period that was a turning point— for the good—in Charlotte's history from the perspectives of both human rights and sound financial business practices. The two mayors who served four terms each left major imprints on the city as it approached the 21st century.

The scores of persons interviewed during the preparation of the book in 1992–1994 reflected that the city's early history also had a major impact on what happened in the

1960s, 1970s and beyond. Former City Manager David Burkhalter was particularly persuasive as he reflected in 1993 on why it all happened the way it did. The genial, white-thatched Burkhalter had played a major role in what occurred during Belk's four terms, but the writing of this history of those years gave him a chance to reconsider that era from a historical viewpoint.

Burkhalter observed that Charlotte really had no reason to exist, not being directly on a major river nor on the ocean. The railroad didn't come until the mid-19th century. Charlotte, or what became Charlotte, had grown from a little settlement or trading post along the paths created by Indians and early settlers. The Scotch-Irish settlers were fiercely independent with firm resolves for independence. When it came time for state government to create a county seat, Thomas Polk and others had raised the money and built a courthouse in Charlotte. That can-do and will-do spirit lived on into the period covered by this book. Railroads, highways, the airport, courthouses, schools, theaters, convention centers and coliseums have been planned and built and made the city what it was in 1994—aspiring to world class status.

The city was ready for what occurred between 1961 and 1977. The end of World War II ended the industrial age, Burkhalter said, and kicked off the information age. State banking laws meshed well with local banking practices.

Stan Brookshire, a man of strong spiritual and ethical convictions along with a great deal of business savvy, was instrumental in removing the major barriers of racial conflict that held back such cities as Birmingham and Montgomery.

Brookshire might well agree with the words of Charles Longstreet Weltner, former Georgia congressman and later judge, who wrote in his 1966 book, *The Southerner:*

"Our fundamental charter declares all men equal. Our basic religion declares us our brother's keeper. But the demand for justice rests not alone on legal precept or theological tenet. It is a demand that spans creed and clan, age and continent. It speaks now as it has to prophet, saint and patriot—and to unnumbered millions of men and women throughout time.

"It wells up from the heart as plain truth and clear duty.

"Let right be done."

Then came John Belk who passionately believed that Charlotte was ready to take advantage of the new era with its challenges and opportunities. Belk's judgment, devotion to the city, sense of integrity and personal magnetism were the hallmarks of his years at City Hall.

Those interviewed for this book were asked to rate Charlotte's most recent nine mayors. Interestingly, the ratings changed very little from the first person interviewed to the last and virtually everyone was close in agreement, at least in the order in which the mayors were ranked. Brookshire and Belk ended up with the best scores by a significant margin.

As others interviewed for the book said time and again, the wisdom of Brookshire and Belk and their knowledge about the people they sought to lead was such that Charlotte did come through the 1960s and 1970s in a unique way, often with less conflict than other cities.

The two were different, yet similar, in that both came out of the business world and were accustomed to making decisions in private and with the support of those who had similar views. While the changes that occurred during Brookshire's eight years were generally in the area of civil rights and urban renewal and thereby generated by him,

Belk was forced to deal with more changes not of his own making. Demands came from women, Republicans, blacks and neighborhood groups that heretofore had not attempted to exercise anywhere near the clout they did beginning in the 1970s.

Decision making was still a closely held matter in 1969, but much less centralized by 1977. A homogeneous leadership group no longer existed and business leaders had to share power with other coalitions to a much greater degree. Few questioned, certainly not openly nor widely, the hand-picking of mayors by a select few in the 1960s. And it should be noted that no serious opposition arose from outside the select circle against Brookshire after he defeated former Councilwoman Martha Evans in 1961. John Tate, who gave Brookshire his only tough political battle, was a banker. Gibson Smith, the only one to really threaten Belk, was a successful real estate man.

One councilman who served in that period observed that the general attitude among his fellow council members was that it was perfectly appropriate for seven men from Southeast Charlotte to get elected, serve, meet in secret and make decisions affecting the entire city—and that those on the westside "should be grateful we were willing to take the time . . . But this would not last with the coming of district representation."

Charlotte was nearly 82 percent Democrat, at least in registration, when Brookshire took office. The Democratic Party registration was down to almost 73 percent by the time Belk took office and just under 68 percent when he left office. In addition, the city's population jumped from 208,780 when Brookshire entered City Hall to 320,000 by the time Belk exited. The black percentage of the city's population was 28 percent when Brookshire entered City

Hall in 1961 and only about a percentage point more when he left in 1969. It was nearly 27 percent when Belk left office in 1977. The Charlotte-Mecklenburg Board of Elections has no breakdown for black-white registration percentages in the 1960s, but reported that blacks made up 18 percent of the registered voters by the time Belk turned over the reins to Ken Harris.

Downtown Charlotte in 1961 looked nothing like it did in 1969 and certainly not like it did in 1977. A large area around what is now Marshall Park was a maze of slums. Charlotte CPA Randy Whitt in 1993 remembered getting lost while working in the area as a young accounting intern for A.M. Pullen & Company in the late 1960s before urban renewal turned the area into what it was in the 1970s and beyond. And the perception (at least, to this young newspaper reporter and his friends) was that the Cotswold Apartments, where many school teachers lived, was so far out of town that a trip there was something to ponder when planning an evening out.

The book is not intended to be a recapitulation of City Council minutes, but the human version of the contributions of Brookshire and Belk. It is not even intended to be a comprehensive report about the Brookshire and Belk years. The book deals with the questions of how and why Charlotte evolved into the business community it did.

Former Tar Heel Governor Luther Hodges may have laid the groundwork with his book *Businessman in the Statehouse*, published in 1962. After explaining how he eliminated some unnecessary bureaucratic red tape soon after he took office in 1954, Hodges wrote: "This was a small matter but it lent credit to a pet theory of mine that sound principles of good business could and should apply to government . . . This small incident . . . was my first effort to make North Carolina state government more efficient and more economical. It was not my last." That could easily have been written by Brookshire and Belk.

Political scientist Schley Lyons of the University of North Carolina at Charlotte said in 1993 that the administrations of Brookshire and Belk were remarkably clean, in contrast to that of other cities. In fact, Lyons said, Charlotte's politics have traditionally been "squeaky clean." He said Brookshire and Belk served out of public obligation, a trait that was disappearing in American politics at all levels. In her 1980 book, *Charlotte: Spirit of the New South*, Mary Norton Kratt wrote, "Whether Charlotte has been kept honest by her heritage, her acumen or by provincial naiveté is debatable. But the effect is open, responsive and often feisty government."

Brookshire and Belk were successful in other fields and decided to "give back" to the community. The current trend is that of professional politicians, whose major goal is simply to hold office. Brookshire, Belk and their kind, on the other hand, saw needs that they believed should be met and offered themselves for office to lead the city to the accomplishment of those goals. "But they are a dying breed," Lyons lamented. The professional class of politicians that dominates politics today, Lyons said, would include such people as North Carolina governors Jim Martin and Jim Hunt and President Bill Clinton.

Neal Peirce, who has written numerous books and columns on state and municipal government, said the phenomenon of the death of the businessman-mayor is global. The power base within cities is much more scattered than in the past, he said, which means local government is more democratic, but less able to get things done.

Peirce, incidentally, had written briefly about Charlotte

in his 1975 book, *The Border South States*. While mentioning that Charlotte was "a city of branch offices, banks, insurance companies, and trucking firms," he wrote that the Queen City "seems to have its eyes constantly on Atlanta; though it will never eclipse that city, it surely will remain the largest in the state . . . But what Charlotte is most known for these days is the Charlotte-Mecklenburg County school desegregation case . . ."

Peirce, notable for his insights as well as the unusual spelling of his last name, directed me to Alan Ehrenhalt, who wrote a book on the subject, *The United States of Ambition*, in 1991. Ehrenhalt wrote of the decline of the power of political parties and local power structures. In years past, a system existed that enabled businessmen to offer for political office when they felt they were best prepared. "Now any fool can run and get elected," Peirce said. Ehrenhalt wrote that people can now "nominate themselves" for office.

Ehrenhalt, in turn, quoted from Robert Dahl's 1961 book, *Who Governs?*, in which Dahl reflected on the same issue, saying that the business communities that produced the Brookshires and Belks in cities like Charlotte had abdicated their roles (Dahl didn't actually cite Charlotte specifically): ". . . the business community was more interested in making money than making policy." Floyd Hunter of the University of North Carolina at Chapel Hill, writing on Atlanta's situation, talked of a network of 40 people who ran that city in the 1950s—a situation, it should be noted, that continued through Mayor Ivan Allen's tenure, which closely paralleled Brookshire's in time and accomplishments. Erhenhalt contended that Hunter was writing of a system that was "about to expire" and Dahl "understood the future."

Ehrenhalt argued in his book that "when it comes to power and authority, as with most other subjects, nostalgia has a way of playing tricks on us." He wrote that the past often seems simpler than it really was and the present "takes on a complexity that the past never seems to have possessed."

The fact remained, however, Ehrenhalt wrote, that few would have thought of themselves as professional politicians in the 1950s (and I would argue in Charlotte for many years past that).

Peirce spoke of the situation in 1993 as a "splinterization of power," in which no one ever has complete power and various groups can checkmate each other. The result, he said, is good and bad, with more groups involved, but less accomplished.

Lyons said the same thing. Belk and Burkhalter hinted at it—and my bet is that Brookshire would have agreed also.

Their kind may not be seen again, but Charlotte is the better for their having served. And now their story . . .

Brookshire & Belk

BUSINESSMEN
IN CITY HALL

Introducing the Era

Whether 1961 is ancient history or just yesterday really depends on how old you are now.

West Side Story was the top movie of the year and Harper Lee won a Pulitzer Prize for *To Kill A Mockingbird*. Don Schwall of Boston was the American League's rookie of the year, Jack Nicklaus was the amateur golfer of the year, Gary Player was the first non-American to win the Masters and Frank McGuire's last University of North Carolina team (before Dean Smith took over) went 19-4 behind Doug Moe and York Larese. Duke beat Arkansas 7-6 in the Cotton Bowl, Ernie Davis of Syracuse won the Heisman Trophy, and Jim Brown was the top rusher and George Blanda was the top passer in the NFL. Roger Maris hit 61 home runs, and Cincinnati was the NCAA basketball champion. Mrs. Edwin Jones scored a hole-in-one on Myers Park Country Club's Number 7 hole. Myers Park High School beat East Mecklenburg 31-0 behind the 250-yard passing effort of junior Jeff Beaver.

Terry Sanford and Ernest Hollings were paid $25,000 and $15,000 respectively as governors of North Carolina and South Carolina, and it cost four cents to mail a first-class letter. Patrice Lumumba was murdered, the Peace

Corps was created, Yuri Gagarin became the first human space traveler, the Cuban invasion failed as did the right-wing rebellion in Algeria, and Dag Hammarskjold was killed in a plane crash.

Most firms in Charlotte were locally owned. Neither the Convention Center, George Shinn's NBA Hornets, Lake Norman, SouthPark or Eastland Mall existed. The Charlotte Checkers hockey team was the city's pro team favorite. Charlottetown Mall (the city's first enclosed mall) was two years old. The population of the city was about 200,000. Cotswold Mall was two years in the future. South Tryon was well on its way in changing from retailing to a financial strip.

Harry Golden was the city's best-known journalist and used Tanner's, a downtown institution, as inspiration for his "Vertical Integration Plan." Brown-bagging was the method whereby one had a mixed drink with a meal in a restaurant. Much of the city was segregated, the Brooklyn slums blighted the city, ministers Carlyle Marney and Warner Hall had influence that no ministers would ever achieve again and only two black children were in schools with whites.

Vietnam was not yet a major controversial issue.

The Charlotte Motor Speedway won a reprieve when foreclosure proceedings were postponed in late October. Julian Scheer was a columnist for *The Charlotte News*. Davidson College celebrated its 125th anniversary. Most men's haircuts cost $1.50. Kenny McArver of Willow Oak Road, a Myers Park High School graduate and a Salem College student, was selected as Miss Charlotte. Mrs. T.J. Myers of Independence Boulevard and her neighbors told City Council that their neighborhood was becoming unfit as a residential area. Piedmont North Carolina farmers were hit by a crippling drought. Purple was the most popular color among high school students, reported Jeff Davis, a Garinger High School senior.

Larry Johnson and Alonzo Mourning hadn't been born yet.

Bill Lee was assistant to the chief engineer at Duke Power Company, Hugh McColl was working for newly created North Carolina National Bank, George Shinn was packaging towels and washcloths for Cannon Mills in Kannapolis, Jim Martin was teaching chemistry at Davidson College, and Johnny Harris was in the eighth grade at Charlotte Country Day School.

At the start of the year, the New Frontier of John F. Kennedy was enthralling the country despite the Bay of Pigs fiasco. Sam Ervin and Everett Jordan were North Carolina's senators while Olin Johnston and Strom Thurmond were serving in the U.S. Senate for the Palmetto state. Charles R. Jonas represented the 10th District in the U.S. House of Representatives after turning back a second challenge by David Clark. James Smith was ending four years as mayor of Charlotte and Stanford R. Brookshire had just been replaced by Joe H. Robinson as president of the Charlotte Chamber of Commerce.

Elmer Rouzer of the Ruddick Corporation was chairman of the Redevelopment Commission, Joe Grier Jr. was chairman of the Parks and Recreation Commission. Elmer Garinger was superintendent of the Charlotte-Mecklenburg schools.

As for future mayors, Ken Harris had graduated from UNC-Chapel Hill four years before and was in the trust department at NCNB; Eddie Knox was in Wake Forest Law School; Harvey Gantt was at Iowa State University; Sue Myrick was working for the Department of the Army in

Port Clinton, Ohio; and Richard Vinroot was a sophomore playing basketball for Dean Smith.

John Belk? He was in charge of the buying office at Belk, where he had a pretty good future.

Part One
Stan Brookshire 1961–1969

What Was Happening Elsewhere

1961 — John F. Kennedy takes office
        Cuban Missile Crisis

1962 — John Glenn first American in orbit
        Craig Phillips succeeds Elmer Garinger as local
        school superintendent
        GOP Chairman William E. Cobb discovered to
        have two families
        Charlotte-Mecklenburg schools get first mobile
        classrooms
        Davidson beats Duke 72–69 in basketball

1963 — Harvey Gantt integrates Clemson College
        Martin Luther King Jr. makes "I Have A
        Dream" speech
        John F. Kennedy assassinated
        Charlotte College becomes four-year school

1964 — Lyndon Johnson routs Barry Goldwater
Gulf of Tonkin Resolution passed

1965 — Malcolm X assassinated
University of North Carolina at Charlotte
created
New York City blackout occurs

1966 — Medicare begins
Edward Brooke first black senator elected in 85
years

1967 — Thurgood Marshall first black United States
Supreme Court justice
Christiaan Barnard performs first successful
heart transplant

1968 — Martin Luther King assassinated
Robert F. Kennedy assassinated
Richard Nixon beats Hubert Humphrey

Chapter One

"No, Not Interested!"

Stanford R. Brookshire had just completed a sometimes controversial term as president of the Charlotte Chamber of Commerce with some relief that it was over and figured that he could now go back to his business, Engineering Sales Company of Charlotte. In his farewell address to the chamber in January 1961, Brookshire spoke of the unfinished business brought on by the "explosive growth after World War II." He emphasized the need for better planning and zoning, new revenue sources, more school classrooms, parks and roads, the clearing of unsightly slums, new hospitals and "a place where jet airliners can take off and land." The chamber's theme during Brookshire's tenure had been "Beauty and Betterment with Growth and Greatness."

Brookshire was born July 22, 1905, in Troutman, North Carolina. He had been managing editor of Duke's student newspaper and moved to Charlotte in 1927, when the city's population was 75,000. He worked as a reporter at *The Charlotte Observer* until a hearing defect forced him to flee the high noise level then common in newspaper city rooms.

The first clipping in *The Charlotte Observer*'s files on Brookshire, who was widely recognized for decades as a major civic force, was from 1952 when he was named to the High Point College Board of Trustees. In 1956, he had headed Charlotte's first $1 million-plus United Way campaign.

Conventional wisdom in 1961 had former Councilwoman Martha Evans—who had fiery red hair to go with a similar personality—ousting James Smith, who was seeking a third term, as mayor. Her credentials were good, especially within certain moderate and liberal camps, and she had—in the words of two old clichés—paid her dues and done her homework. Interesting as a sign of the times was a newspaper report that referred to her as "a gay and provocative gal." Evans had come within 926 votes of beating Smith two years before. Smith was given virtually no chance of winning a third term because he had moved his business to Gastonia and was being criticized for lack of leadership.

But the Charlotte business community, which was far more cohesive and powerful than it would be 30 years later, wasn't content to let Evans move into the mayor's position. The consensus was that Charlotte was not ready for a woman as mayor, certainly not one with liberal leanings. The power structure members looked around for another candidate. Virtually no one openly objected to the process being handled by white males meeting in private. Nor did the media cover the process as thoroughly as would have happened a generation later.

Brookshire, in his family history, "Brookshire Lives," put it this way: "To the political observers and the business and civic leadership, it seemed obvious that Mrs. Evans, a capable but fiery redhead, having built a strong political base (particularly among the minority groups) during her two terms on council, would win over the field. The business and civic leadership of Charlotte was not happy with such a prospect."

Several asked Brookshire if he would run. "No, not interested," he said. He said later he expected to support S. Herbert Hitch, then a councilman, in a run for mayor. Hitch instead ran for another council term and was edged off the council by newcomer Don Bryant who had been recruited to run by J. Murrey Atkins, president of R.S. Dickson & Company.

Brookshire did accept Atkins' request to attend a strategy meeting on the mayoral situation only three-and-a-half weeks before the primary. Atkins was a friend and former college classmate of Brookshire at Duke University. When Brookshire got to Atkins' office, about 20 men (then it was only men who were invited to such things) were in the conference room—totally committed to Brookshire's candidacy. They told Brookshire they would help him with "a fast and hard campaign" and would raise all the campaign expenses. It would cost Brookshire nothing. Atkins and most others at that meeting have since died, and the other details have vanished from the memories of those who survive.

Brookshire had shown signs that he was more progressive on certain issues than the majority of those present, but was not the moderate-liberal or liberal-moderate that Evans was. While he was definitely in synch with the chamber philosophy, Brookshire had to deny during the campaign that he was the chamber's hand-picked candidate. Both *The Charlotte News* and *The Charlotte Observer* endorsed him.

Brookshire agreed to be the business candidate to guard the gates of City Hall against Evans, but only if all of those gathered promised not to come to him for favors once he sat in the mayor's chair. In his family history, Brookshire said he told his friends he "would be under no obligation to them individually or collectively. I didn't want any of them, if I were elected, coming to City Hall and saying they elected me and wanted a favor. They agreed, and I announced my candidacy a few days later. Let me say, to their credit, that none of them ever asked a favor."

Among the hundreds of letters in the Brookshire files of the UNC Charlotte archives is a letter from John Belk saying that he was pleased Brookshire was in the race and referring to their golfing together. Industrialist Oliver Rowe declined to be Brookshire's campaign manager, citing his (Rowe's) inexperience, but Democratic Party powers Paul Younts, Tom Little and Dwight Phillips did help run the campaign. The three worked behind the scenes and while the news media knew who they were, the general public was probably not aware of their extensive involvement and interest.

After only a 14-day campaign, Brookshire led the balloting with 8,242 votes to 7,619 for Evans. James Smith, who drew criticism from both for moving his business and for allowing City Council, not the mayor, to take a leadership role in the selection process of a police chief and city manager, had only 2,108. Former veteran City Councilman Jim Whittington recalls Smith's losing his place in the text during a debate with Brookshire as newsman Doug Mayes monitored the debate. Former City Attorney Henry Yancey was eliminated in the primary as was Smith. After another week of campaigning, Brookshire led the runoff over Evans by 15,905 to 13,133. The UNC Charlotte files show that Brookshire paid WSOC-TV a mere $251.53 for ten 10-second campaign spots used during the primary race.

In this election, but none of the others in which

Brookshire or John Belk ran, the majority of the black vote went to the opponent. Evans' credentials enabled her to carry a majority of the black boxes. It was said later that Evans' support of black issues nudged Brookshire to be a bit more progressive once he was in office. And it also was suggested that Brookshire, because he wasn't publicly known to have strong black support, could get away with moving faster on racial issues than if the white community had suspected him of paying off political debts. The UNC Charlotte archives show that Brookshire spent only $625.63 with WSOC-TV between the primary and election for six 10-second, one 20-second, and three 60-second ads.

Charlotte at the time elected its city officials in a very strange way. A non-partisan primary nominated two mayoral candidates and 14 council candidates for the election a week later. The mayor and seven council members were elected in that general election. In 1961, the mayor and all council members, as well as all members of the legislative delegation, were Democrats.

∞

Brookshire, who was only 5 feet 8 inches tall, had a high energy level and the characteristic of rising on his toes as he spoke in staccato bursts. He also had an unmistakable and distinct voice inflection. Years later, veteran radio and television newsman Doug Mayes called it "almost a stutter." Others said it seemed as if Brookshire were about to pronounce the last syllable of long words twice. He had trouble with some words, such as "circumferential." A top city official of that time recalled an occasion when City Council was to honor hospital volunteers called "Candy Stripers." Brookshire misread the agenda item and demanded to know why the city was honoring "Candy Strippers" and wanted to know what they did—"Did they strip?"

Not a good driver, Brookshire had more than his share of fender benders, several recalled years later.

A humble man, he would say "compliments are like perfume—to be smelled, not swallowed." And while not known for his sense of humor, he was virtually always up to speed on the subjects he dealt with.

Richard Vinroot, Charlotte's mayor when interviewed, grew up with Stanford Brookshire Jr. Vinroot recalled the senior Brookshire as "an authoritarian figure, but I remember being impressed that my boyhood friend was the son of the man who was mayor." Sue Myrick, who was to follow Brookshire in the mayor's office 18 years after he left, agreed that Brookshire was "always a gentleman, a good person with a big heart." When interviewed after Brookshire died of lung cancer in 1990, Myrick said Brookshire was "a giant . . . a soft-spoken Christian."

∞

So Brookshire got the job that paid $3,600, yet was in no way as time-consuming as it became in later years. The city budget was then $16.5 million and $32 million by the time Brookshire left office.

After his election, Brookshire promised improvement in race relations and a strong program of redevelopment of Brooklyn, the slum at the edge of the downtown commercial area, and proposed that a government plaza be built there. Brookshire called for a new police building within five years and construction of new fire stations. He also urged movement on the plan to eliminate the Southern Railroad grade crossing on West Trade Street, to add signaling at 71 intersections in the central business district, and to construct the Northwest Expressway.

Because the staunch conservative Republican Charles R. Jonas represented Charlotte in Congress throughout the

Brookshire years, Brookshire was called the "congressman without portfolio" in certain circles. Brookshire described his role in this way in his family history: "One of the more important and time-consuming things I did while in office was to cultivate the sources of these (federal) funds in Washington, in which I think I was more than moderately successful. At least, I am satisfied that Charlotte got its share in those years, and should have because we pay our share of the federal take. Two people in Washington were most helpful, Vice President Hubert Humphrey, whom the President (Johnson) named a liaison man with municipalities, and Presidential Assistant Henry Hall Wilson, whose friendship as well as help I valued highly."

Brookshire wrote that after a Rose Garden bill-signing ceremony, Wilson asked if he could do anything for Brookshire. The mayor said he'd like some money for water-and-sewer acquisition, which was provided for in the bill just signed. Brookshire said Wilson called an official in the U.S. Department of Housing and Urban Development and said the mayor of Charlotte was coming to the HUD office "in 15 minutes—give him whatever he wants." Charlotte got $1.5 million of the $100 million in the bill.

In his first year, Brookshire adopted a workable, businesslike budget with a broadened approach to pay-as-you-go financing. He consistently fought for that principle and angered some council members by calling for reconsideration of $500,000 in pay-as-you-go funds cut out by council in 1964.

∞

In 1963, about 15 percent of the voters turned out to give Brookshire his second term. His only opposition was Albert T. Pearson, who failed to cause Brookshire any worry whatsoever. In fact, on one occasion Brookshire couldn't even remember Pearson's name and referred to his opponent at a council meeting as "Albert What's-His-Name?" The vote after a very quiet campaign was 7,634 to 3,353. Every incumbent council member was reelected.

Six months later, rumors circulated that Brookshire had already decided not to seek a third term. Nor was he interested in challenging Republican Congressman Jonas as had been suggested.

Yet after four years, Brookshire had been awarded an honorary degree by Pfeiffer College, had been named Man of the Year by *The Charlotte News* for 1964 and was serving as president of the North Carolina League of Municipalities. He only agreed to run after Whittington was widely suggested as his successor. Whittington, who served as mayor pro tempore for most of his tenure on council and was a powerful member of that body, was to serve on council from the spring of 1957 until he was defeated for mayor in 1977. But Brookshire never saw him as a fitting man for the mayor's chair. Ten days before the primary, Councilman Gibson Smith filed to run for mayor, but Whittington was smart enough to see the political writing on the wall and stuck to the council race.

(On a personal note, in my research in the UNC Charlotte archives I found a letter I wrote to Brookshire to urge him to run again. Brookshire answered that he would, but expected me to return from Washington, where I was working for Jonas, to vote for him. I did.)

Brookshire beat Smith in the 1965 primary 13,593 to 5,803. Pearson, making another try for the top spot, got 1,970. C.C. Beasley received 474 votes and William C. McIntire got 145. In the election itself, Brookshire got 18,432 to Smith's 9,258. Because Smith was so much better known than Pearson had been two years previously, the turnout more than doubled that of 1963. Yet Smith offered no dramatic change in that he, too, came from the same general business background as had Brookshire. Brookshire charged Smith with injecting racism into the campaign and Smith said "kingmakers," whom he did not name publicly, had bought Negro votes on Brookshire's behalf. Brookshire beat Smith 5,368 to 177 in the all-black precincts.

Fred Alexander, who later was to lead the council ticket, squeaked in to capture the seventh council seat and become the first black to sit on City Council. According to Mary Snead Boger, the author of *Charlotte 23*, Dr. J.T. Williams, a black man, had served on the Board of Aldermen years before by virtue of being a member of the Committee on City Education. And, in 1934, Alexander almost got a black elected to the 11-member City Council. That scared white Charlotte sufficiently so that the General Assembly changed the method of electing city councilmen, eliminating the ward system and reducing the council from 11 to seven members. Alexander employed the "single-shot" method of getting elected in 1965, much to the chagrin of several other council candidates, who counted on black votes to win. Single-shot voting meant a voter cast only one vote in the council races, not the seven he or she was entitled to.

∞

Brookshire announced a five-point program just after the 1965 election. It included development of the expressway system with emphasis on the central loop, slum clearance, enforcement of the minimum housing code, widening of downtown streets—especially Third, Fourth, Sixth, and Brevard streets—and city beautification.

By 1967, Brookshire was again touted as a possible opponent of Jonas, but instead decided to run again for mayor. He said his major reason was that he wanted to be around for Charlotte's bicentennial celebration in 1968. (He named John Belk as chairman of the celebration committee.) Another unstated reason was that he simply didn't want Whittington to be mayor of Charlotte. When interviewed for this book, Whittington said he thought 1967 had offered him his best chance to be mayor. But banker John A. "Jack" Tate Jr., a last-minute candidate and Brookshire's good friend, almost took the fourth term away from Brookshire, finishing only 43 votes behind in an election that saw 36 percent of the eligible voters go to the polls. Brookshire's total was 15,833 and Tate's was 15,790. Brookshire had been the third Charlotte mayor to serve three terms. Now he became the first to serve four terms.

Tate said in 1993 that he had thought Brookshire was a good mayor the first term, showing "vigor and enthusiasm." He was almost as effective the second term, but things were "old hat" by the third term. "At times I thought he was slowing progress," Tate, who had been active in the development of the 1966 Master Plan, recalled. A significant number of voters apparently agreed with Tate and presumably thought it was time for a new face in City Hall. And, it should be noted again, Tate wasn't seen as a major change, having been a successful banker and civic leader. Tate said he had become so frustrated with government that he took an abbreviated course in government at the Institute of Government in Chapel Hill. The problem was that his history lesson showed him that the founding fathers had created a government form that made making decisions difficult. Tate was echoing a sentiment similar to what Robert F. Kennedy said as he campaigned for the presidency in 1968 shortly before he was assassinated: "Moral courage is a rarer commodity than bravery in battle or great intelligence. Yet it is the one essential, vital quality for those who seek to change a world that yields most painfully to change."

Brookshire might have stepped aside for Tate had the banker not waited until after Brookshire filed for the fourth term. Writing to me in April 1967, Brookshire said he expected "a high level campaign with complete absence of mud slinging. If I do not win the election, at least I will get out from under some heavy responsibilities and have considerable more time for my family, my business, for gardening and for golf." But the campaign got a bit nasty, at least for Charlotte in those days, although Tate said years later he disagreed with that assessment. The two candidates said nothing that was unkind or personal, he argued. At the time, Tate charged that Brookshire was soft on crime. After six years as mayor, Brookshire had lost some of the support he once had within the business community and among council members. *The Charlotte News* endorsed Brookshire, but *The Charlotte Observer* said either Brookshire or Tate would make a good mayor.

Attorney James McMillan, who later was to give Mayor John Belk fits as a federal judge by holding up various projects, was Tate's campaign manager. Brookshire, who traditionally had won the votes of the richest and poorest of Charlotte voters, was matched vote for vote by Tate in the so-called silk stocking precincts. Tate took a majority of the middle- and lower-income white votes—and may have captured a majority of the white votes, but Brookshire did much better in black precincts.

Former City Councilman Milton Short recalled years later that Brookshire hired and paid poll workers, rather than seek volunteers from within the Democratic Party. Brookshire told Short at the time that he simply didn't want to take the time to recruit the volunteers. Short said he was amused at some of the extremely well-dressed women who showed up at the polls to support Brookshire. "I guess they were Kelly girls," Short said. One person, who viewed the election closely, said that Brookshire's campaign manager, banker Charlie Smith, spent money in the black community without knowing how it was being spent and, hence, the effort did not achieve the desired purpose. Smith later was to die in a plane crash while working for gubernatorial candidate Rufus Edmisten.

It was said that boxes were bought until the 1960s and early 1970s. The way it worked was that money was paid to the bag man and his helpers, who would go in to vote early, taking the paper ballot (this was before voting machines were installed) out to hand to the next voter. That voter was given $1 or so and told how to vote on the ballot and to bring his or her ballot out so the process could be repeated.

Brookshire was to write later in his family history that "Jack and I were good friends before the election and are still friendly. We belong to the same city and country clubs, and we divided votes among mutual friends, even in some families. For example, Mrs. Eddie Jones told her invalid husband at breakfast on the day of the election that she was going to vote for Jack Tate. Mr. Jones responded by saying that if she did, he was going to get dressed and go vote for Stan Brookshire—and he did!"

Betty Chafin Rash, who later served as a council member for three terms, recalled in 1993 that she voted for Tate, "but I'm not sure why. Maybe it was because he seemed more youthful." Tate was 50, almost a dozen years younger.

Tate's slogan: "The President can have only two terms, the Governor only one, why should the mayor have four terms?"

After the election, James McMillan called then City Attorney James W. Kiser (corporate counsel and secretary for NationsBank in 1994) at home on a Sunday afternoon to ask about the possibility of a recount. Kiser explained that a state statute did govern such things, but required a formal process, involving charges of fraud and/or other serious irregularities. McMillan asked Kiser if it didn't bother him that some might not agree with his interpretation. Kiser said it did bother him, particularly when an attorney such as McMillan disagreed, but, nevertheless, that was his (Kiser's) interpretation. Later, Kiser reported the call to the Board of Elections and repeated his interpretation of the state statute. When Tate and McMillan did not pursue the request for a recount, the elections board, headed by Liz Hair at that time, did not order one. In a prepared statement, Hair said that no recount would be held "unless significant discrepancies are shown in the course of the canvass." When interviewed for this book, Tate said the decision not to have a recount was "a sour note," but would not elaborate.

Someone who was active in the Tate campaign remembered that the last boxes to come in were from a black precinct, and suspected foul play because of Brookshire's wide margin in that precinct. The Tate supporter also recalled the feeling in some quarters that it would not be "proper" for Tate to challenge Brookshire with a recount. "It was some sort of Southern thing that it would be bad for the city," he said. "I don't know what information they had, because they didn't talk to me about specifics," Kiser said a quarter of a century later. But, he added, some Tate supporters thought there might be irregularities. McMillan said at the time that his plea for a recount was not based on charges of irregularities "since proof would be a serious offense" and Tate had no desire to launch a "wholesale investigation." Kiser said he admired Tate for not pursuing something that might have seriously divided the city.

Although Tate said years later that the loss probably was a blessing because he went on to successfully head a Davidson bank, he admitted he was unwilling to reveal all his thoughts about the election. Indications were that he still harbored some disappointment, even if he did say "it was no great calamity." Being mayor without any other job would have cost him thousands of dollars, he said. "The Lord was looking after me. It would have been very expensive for me (to be mayor) . . . The last 15 to 20 years of my business career were happy, productive and pleasant. The people did me a favor."

Tate, the man who almost was mayor, said a quarter century later that Brookshire "was a man of good will, an upbeat person, progressive . . . Stan was basically a fine mayor—for the first and second terms." Some voters, but not enough to win him the election, agreed with Tate.

Ironically, Whittington outpolled them both, getting 5,500 more votes in the council race. Claude Albea, first elected in 1931, lost this time. Except for 1945 to 1947, he had been on council since his initial victory. Albea was a pleasant, sincere man, about whom it was said he had "one year's experience 34 times." And Gibson Smith was re-elected to council after his unsuccessful bid for the mayor's chair in 1965.

Years later, Harvey Gantt, mayor in 1983–1987, said Brookshire was the last mayor to avoid "the sting of a changing population." John Belk, who followed Brookshire, faced partisan challenges as well as more insistent demands from women, blacks and neighborhood groups.

Chapter Two

The People and How They Got Along

Charlotte had and has a "weak mayor" form of government. The mayor had no important appointive powers and was able to vote only in cases of ties. Brookshire, however, was called a strong mayor after only a year in office. Yet he struggled to offer strong leadership without stepping on toes. Brookshire was accused of not confiding in council members and of giving his opinion on issues Charlotte mayors traditionally had kept out of.

"Stan wanted to stand apart from council," former City Councilman John Thrower (who served during 1961–67 and 1969–71) recalled in 1993. "He was never a council person. Quite frankly, he had to be reminded that decisions were not his alone. He always considered himself the Chamber of Commerce's choice for mayor and he ran the city from that perspective." Thrower said he remembered Brookshire once decided that city parks should be closed at 10 p.m. and instructed the city attorney to draw up an ordinance to that effect. "He didn't have the authority to do that. He should have recommended that it be done. But we had to sit down with the ordinance in front of us," Thrower said.

W.J. "Bill" Veeder, who was to serve as city manager throughout Brookshire's four terms, observed in 1993 that he didn't think Brookshire ever "knowingly tried to circumvent the council members, but he did try to influence them . . . Many things were initiated by Brookshire. They (council members) may have wished later they had thought of these things."

Brookshire often had good answers ready even before the council had the questions, but "he didn't ignore them (council members). He spent a lot of time with them individually. He worked diligently with them. They just wanted to be consulted even more," Veeder said.

Soon after being elected, Brookshire reported to council that the city had a business-like budget and a broader approach to pay-as-you-go financing. Brookshire and Veeder successfully got council to adopt a five-year pay-as-you-go capital budget in 1961. Former Assistant City Manager William H. "Bill" Carstarphen recalled that the city budget was only about $20 million when he came to work in City Hall in 1964 and that he and Paul Bobo, another assistant city manager, used to hide out in a basement office in mid-April and emerge 30 days later with the budget prepared for council's consideration. "There was no budget office then," he said.

The Brookshire-Belk years saw major improvement in the way city government approached financial matters.

Brookshire was not a political mayor in the classical sense and was never known to be active in Democratic Party activities. Just before his death, he told a television reporter that he "was one of the most unpolitical mayors Charlotte ever had" and that his successor John Belk fit that mold also.

Former County Commission Chairman Charles M. Lowe, who served on the County Commission off and on during the 1950s, 1960s and 1970s, called Brookshire "a good man and a dear man."

While most gave Brookshire high marks for being the consummate Southern gentleman, one former elected county official, who worked with Brookshire on several issues, said he was not easy to talk with and not receptive to new ideas. This person, when interviewed for this book, asked not to be identified, but said John Belk was far easier to deal with. This was a rare opinion, however.

Sue Myrick, who served as mayor in 1987–91, said she believed time will prove that Brookshire had a greater effect on the city than people thought then or even a quarter century later. "He was so forward-thinking," she said.

Myrick said Brookshire was helpful to her as she developed strategy for her political career. "I talked to him a lot and he was very supportive," she recalled in early 1993. "We had a good relationship. He gave me insights into the workings of government." Myrick said she and Brookshire also kept in touch after her election as mayor.

"He was my first impression of a mayor and still in many ways is the best mayor I have ever worked with," said Carstarphen, assistant city manager under Brookshire and Belk, and later city manager in Spartanburg. Carstarphen was Greensboro's city manager in 1994.

"As a person he was incredibly polite and a very sincere individual in his personal relations with people. A Christian, he really projected those values that word means. He was gentle and caring," Carstarphen said. "But he also was a good businessman and fairly shrewd and used that shrewdness in managing council. They had a respect for him and the power he had." Carstarphen said he and Brookshire hit it off immediately, in part because Brookshire and Carstarphen's father (and, coincidentally, mine too) had been at Duke University in the mid-to-late 1920s.

"He was a wonderful mayor, reserved and dignified, a true leader in terms of leading council," said Henry Underhill, who was assistant city attorney beginning in 1965, acting city attorney in 1968 and city attorney through the writing of this book. Underhill said Brookshire was adept in keeping a "focus on his vision . . . and was able to lead without stirring up friction while he worked hard at consensus building."

John Morrisey, who was city attorney in the early 1960s, recalled Brookshire as having a great deal of ability in working with people so the results he sought were obtained, yet was never reluctant to share the credit. "He was a true gentleman and a super guy. I used to look forward to meeting with him," Morrisey said.

Ann Marsh, who worked closely with Brookshire as a receptionist and secretary, said he was "the epitome of a gentleman. I never heard him even raise his voice. He was never frivolous, but always gracious and businesslike." She recalled that once someone brought in a big tub of toasted pecans as a gift to the mayor and the office staff started nibbling away. "We couldn't stay out of them and soon we had eaten half of them. But he never said anything even though I know he knew what had happened." Brookshire was known to bring small gifts back to the office staff from trips he made. The staff would hang their Christmas stockings on a mantle in the mayor's office (Councilman Fred Alexander later was to play Santa Claus every year), and Marsh still had her own stocking hanging in her office just before she retired in 1993. She also recalled that Councilman Steve Dellinger always had chocolate candy in his pockets to pass out to the mayor's staff.

Brookshire loved sweets, but also was a chain-smoker. When his family and doctor urged him to cut back, he switched to small cigars.

∞

The mayor's office was moved from the old City Hall to the Government Center while Myrick was mayor, and she attempted to make sure that Brookshire and his predecessors were remembered through a plaque in the old mayor's office. The plaque, however, has disappeared, perhaps taken down when a movie was shot in the office. The office itself was unused and stayed locked. But it remained nicely, if sparsely, furnished with a beautiful rug, attractive sofa, chairs and desk. A hornet's nest was on the wall behind the desk. The mantle over the fireplace was still there, in stark contrast to the modern office Mayor Richard Vinroot occupied in 1994.

∞

Even though Brookshire never gave any indication that he thought veteran Councilman Jim Whittington was a suitable successor to himself as mayor, Thrower said he believed that Whittington was Brookshire's strongest ally on the council. When interviewed for this book Veeder said that Brookshire counted on Whittington because he could almost always deliver "a couple of votes other than his own." For his part, Whittington years later termed Brookshire "an excellent mayor." He did not deny the common knowledge that Brookshire was never comfortable with Whittington's style.

One councilman of that era, who pleaded not to be identified, said that "(while) I think Whittington liked Stan, the common feeling was that Stan was afraid Whittington might be mayor and he didn't want him to because Whittington wasn't a college graduate and because Brookshire thought Whittington wouldn't be graceful and cultured as a mayor of Charlotte should be." This person also commented that Brookshire liked General Paul Younts, one of the area's Democratic powers, but not Ray King, who served as county party chairman for many years. Brookshire feared that King would exercise too much influence on Whittington if he were elected.

Councilman Don Bryant, who was first elected in 1961, said the 1961–65 councils had three factions—the mayor; himself as the "loyal opposition"; and the other six councilmen, who were generally cohesive in their thoughts.

Bryant characterized Steve Dellinger as perhaps the most effective of the council members and Gibson Smith as perhaps the smartest. Veeder years later called Dellinger "the last of a breed . . . who had contacts throughout the city . . . He was likable personally, but could be super tough." Another elected official of that era called Dellinger a "pistol and a problem." Smith could be "a loose cannon and could be vindictive at times," one old hand at City Hall said years later. A long-time city staffer called Smith "a street fighter. If you crossed him, he'd get you."

Bryant said he usually was "in synch" with Brookshire. And it was no secret that there was no love lost between Bryant and Whittington, who were rivals in the funeral business. Although Whittington said he and Bryant "never agreed much, he (Bryant) was a good city councilman." Carstarphen said "even when Bryant opposed you, he was nice about it."

Veeder, who saw a lot of council members come and go, gave his highest marks to Randy Babcock—who served before Brookshire entered City Hall—Fred Alexander and Bryant. Babcock, Veeder said, could get to the heart of an issue quicker than any other council members whom he observed. Alexander was the "consummate councilman . . . a pragmatist . . . a great negotiator." Bryant, although a staunch conservative, had "motives as pure as the driven snow . . . He never had a political agenda; he had a community agenda . . . He related well to Brookshire because they had common community and social backgrounds."

Years later, Veeder said that Councilman Milton Short, who served during the Brookshire and Belk years, was an extremely hard worker and did his homework more completely than any other councilman. Both he and Carstarphen recalled Short's extensive collection of files. But another veteran city official said Short at times was "overly prepared and sometimes was left at the gate."

∞

Bryant said during the 1963 elections, the seven council members agreed that they'd run independently, but have no campaign literature. When they went to the polls, they discovered Whittington had poll workers who were distributing campaign literature. In the voting, Whittington led the ticket, Bryant was second and Smith third.

When the council members gathered at *The Charlotte Observer*, as was then the custom on election night, "the others were livid (at Whittington)," Bryant recalled. Although tradition was that the top vote-getter would be selected mayor pro tempore, it wasn't law. "I suggested Gib (Smith), but the others started hemming and hawing. I guess they were scared of him (Whittington)." Whittington said 30 years later that an overly zealous campaign worker overstepped himself and caused the problem, which Whittington said was "quickly resolved" subsequently at a private meeting at Dellinger's lake cottage.

A veteran at City Hall said years later that Whittington knew the birthdays of every city employee and when one of them got a raise, he or she also got a congratulatory letter from Whittington.

∞

At its first meeting in 1961, City Council reelected Veeder, a strong-willed, 38-year-old hold-over from the James Smith administration, as city manager at $17,500. One cannot understand the Brookshire administration without recognizing the major role played by Veeder, a thoroughly professional government official. Veeder was to remain through a portion of the Belk administration also. In interviews for this book several veteran politicians gave almost as much credit to Veeder as they did to Brookshire and Belk in fashioning Charlotte into the successful, livable city they saw it as being.

Yet shortly after the 1961 election and before the new council members took office, a so-called "reliable source," who asked not to be identified in this book or elsewhere, said that all council members—but not Brookshire—had been called to a secret meeting at Councilman Dellinger's home. The purpose? To find a way to fire Veeder. Whittington, Dellinger, and Claude Albea, hold-overs from the previous council, were still smarting at the way Veeder and Police Chief Jesse James (yes, that was his name) had been hired by the Better Government or "Big Four" slate of Randy Babcock, Brevard Myers, Herbert Hitch and Gib Smith, all of whom had been hand picked by businessman Rush S. Dickson in 1959. The results of the 1961 election were that Hitch, Myers and Babcock were gone and Smith was the only member of the original group left. But he had already proved his independence by the time the election came around again.

"The first thing is we gotta get rid of Veeder," one councilman reportedly said as the meeting began. Several members of the new council vowed to watch Veeder very closely and fire him when he made his first mistake. But the no-nonsense Veeder was too good for them and they never found anything to justify getting rid of him. Veeder subsequently left to work for Pat Hall at Carowinds in 1971. Ironically, Dellinger made the motion in 1961 to reappoint Veeder and Albea seconded it. Whittington, when interviewed more than 30 years later, said he didn't recall Veeder being the object of the council's scrutiny, but did say that the remaining council members were not happy at the way Chief James was hired out of Burlington by the Better Government slate without consultation with other council members.

∞

City Attorney Henry Underhill said Veeder was instrumental in helping him move from assistant city attorney under James Kiser to acting city attorney and eventually city attorney. "I was only 27 and finally went to Bill and formally applied," Underhill said in 1993. "I wondered when you would do it," Veeder said to Underhill. Veeder then told Underhill he had delayed saying anything because he wanted Underhill to come to the decision on his own. Veeder advised Underhill that the handling of a proposed public accommodations ordinance would be the major test on which council members would base their decision about him. Veeder said that Jim Whittington particularly thought Underhill was too young. Underhill said he was pleased that it was Whittington who subsequently made the motion to promote him to city attorney.

∞

Whittington and Councilman John Thrower agreed

that Brookshire and Veeder worked very, very closely, and Thrower added that he thought Veeder "was the best city manager we ever had or will have." It should be noted that Veeder was city manager during Thrower's entire time of service on council. Milton Short, former city councilman, said that Brookshire "readily understood that he was no pro and might say the wrong thing about municipal government. So he totally depended on Veeder and respected him."

Thrower said he even recommended Veeder as a candidate for Congress after the city manager had left Carowinds and gone to work for the Charlotte Chamber of Commerce, but nothing came of the suggestion. Short, when interviewed just before President Bill Clinton was inaugurated in January 1993, said that if Clinton asked him for advice, he'd suggest Veeder for a high federal government position. "He is such a capable man with good judgment and able to make timely decisions . . . He was so strong in his opinions, he had damned well be right—and he was," Short said. He said Veeder would go eyeball-to-eyeball with his bosses—City Council members—behind closed doors.

Veeder also drew high marks from Bryant who said Veeder took City Hall's systems from the dark ages to modern times. "He did an unbelievable job. He was very talented and professional. He was always prepared. I never found him wanting. He was as responsible as Brookshire for the good things that happened in the city." It was during Bryant's term as chairman of the Charlotte Chamber several years later that Veeder was hired for the top staff position at the chamber. Morrisey said Veeder made great use of the University of North Carolina Institute of Government and the North Carolina League of Municipalities and not only was "a great city manager, but a super guy."

One veteran city employee, who worked closely with both Veeder and his successor David Burkhalter, said that "with Veeder you knew what was expected of you and he expected a lot—nothing but the best. He never yelled at me, but he yelled at others. With Burkhalter, I never got any direction. I didn't know what was expected of me. But that was good, because I learned self-discipline. I learned you had to set your own straight and narrow. So it was good."

Veeder was described in a newspaper report at the time as "disciplined in mind and manner."

One person, who occupied a high position in city government for many years but who asked not to be named, said his first encounter with Veeder had hardly begun in the city manager's office when the phone rang and Veeder snatched it up, growling, "What the hell do you want?" It stunned Veeder's guest, who said years later Veeder obviously knew somehow exactly who was calling. This same person, a few years later, had occasion to deal often with Burkhalter and said he rarely knew where Burkhalter stood even after the two discussed an issue.

Those who worked for the sometimes acerbic Veeder said that when you dealt with him, you always knew exactly where you stood, but you also had better know exactly what you wanted from him. His mind worked exceedingly fast and he left little time for small talk. One former reporter said he thought Veeder was too much of a loner and that this hampered him somewhat as a city manager. But this view was shared by few others.

Bill Guerrant, who joined city government just eight months before Veeder left, said the city manager was "a real taskmaster . . . He was difficult to work for." But Guerrant admitted he was involved in starting a new function—public information—and this ran contrary to the Veeder style. Veeder had been known to yell at reporters and come close to physically throwing them out of his office. "He ran a tight ship," Guerrant said, and added that Veeder was reminiscent of generals Guerrant had worked with in Vietnam and subsequently in his military experiences.

Yet, Guerrant said, Veeder's style was common in that time and perhaps was what was needed. Opening up government was "messy and time consuming" and that was definitely not Veeder's way of managing city government.

For his part, Veeder said years later that "Brookshire was no politician, but a businessman who understood change and how to work within a system. He understood the dynamics of working with people. We hit it off very quickly. There was not a day that we didn't talk. We met every morning and talked two or three times during the day. We recognized each other's role and it was very helpful. I understood his policy-making role and he understood the management role of the city manager. It worked *so* well. He never hesitated to share his thoughts on any initiative he undertook."

∞

Veeder incidentally, was never known to lie to the media, but he likewise was never known for cooperating either. He was perhaps the worst source I had in my 17 years as a newsman. But he did have an excellent sense of humor and we traded practical jokes over a 30-year span. Once, upon hearing that secretary Ann Marsh's pet chicken (Yes, that's right, she had adopted the chicken after it fell off a truck.) had been killed by her dog, he brought her several bantam hens, which proceeded to run around her City Hall office.

∞

Betty Chafin Rash, who served three terms on council

during the Belk, Ken Harris and Eddie Knox administrations, said in 1993 that Assistant City Manager Bill Carstarphen had "superb people skills and was a wonderful buffer for Veeder. People felt more comfortable with him . . . but he had the confidence of Veeder."

∞

The mayor and council in the early-to-mid-1960s met in the mayor's office at 2 p.m. for a 60-minute informal session before council meetings. The media was allowed in, but not the public. And reporters were in by the skin of their collective teeth with the gentleman's (no women then) agreement that they were to be circumspect in what they reported. That is, harsh language on the part of councilmen was not be put in print or aired. In May of 1965 Brookshire moved the sessions down the hall to a conference room. Eventually, newsmen were banned from the meeting, primarily because of the tough questioning and reporting by Pat Stith of *The Charlotte Observer*, according to the memory of Doug Smith, who was with *The Charlotte News* for many years and was a business writer at *The Charlotte Observer* in 1994.

Public relations executive Joe Epley, who was a television reporter in that era, believes the changes came after he and his colleagues tried to bring television cameras into the informal sessions. Veeder said years later that he didn't even remember barring the media, but many newsmen of that era do recall being ousted. They just couldn't agree on the details.

Decisions were also known to be made informally in Veeder's office between the session in the mayor's office and the regular council meeting. Morrisey recalled years later that council members often had a question to ask Veeder privately, but that they didn't want to air it publicly.

Council members also gathered in Veeder's office after council meetings. No one, media or public, was allowed in.

Brookshire's office hours generally were 11–12:30 or 1 p.m., but he spent considerable time on city business outside the office, making 15 to 25 appearances a week as mayor. By 1968, the mayor's salary was $5,000 and Brookshire estimated he spent 40 to 50 hours on the job each week.

The Charlotte City Council itself typically would meet several hours on Monday afternoons but set some sort of record when it met for only 17 minutes at a regular meeting October 4, 1966.

∞

The council met secretly about twice a year at the home of council members. There was no law against it at the time, but neither the media nor the public knew of the strategy sessions, held primarily to deal with "some pretty delicate things," recalled Bryant years later. Brookshire attended the gatherings, but Veeder did not. Short said the meetings continued after he came onto council and Bryant left. He said the sessions, held several times a year, sometimes were in a building behind his house and sometimes at Brookshire's house. Elaborate plans were made to keep the news media from finding out about the sessions, which, it should again be noted, were not illegal at that time. In addition, Short recalled years later, smaller groups of council members got together several times a month to discuss controversial matters and to make sure that they'd stick together. He said that stopped during Belk's administration. "My attitude changed," Short said. "We were being screamed at and the General Assembly was getting involved, so I decided to just go down to the meetings and say what I had to say."

∞

Veeder announced a full-scale investigation into the fire department in early 1962 after charges were made that Fire Chief Donald Charles had used off-duty firemen to do work around his house. Charles countered that it was a long-standing, accepted practice. Veeder's report recommended that Charles be given a "severe reprimand" and that the Charlotte Firefighters Association be banned because it was operating essentially as a labor union. Council concurred on both points and approved Veeder's report.

∞

Early in his administration Brookshire complained that he had been left out of the loop in the hiring of Police Chief John Hord, who had been assistant chief. Newcomer Bryant was the only council member to cast a vote against Hord. He had favored John C. "Jake" Goodman, who would later become chief. Hord took over for Jesse James, who had left to work for a division of Florida Steel. Some said at the time that James was nudged out by council members.

After Hord and six other policemen were indicted by the Mecklenburg Grand Jury in November 1964, council granted them leaves of absence for more than a month. Assistant Chief Ernest Selvey was named to replace Hord in the interim. Selvey had been chief for eight months in 1958 after Chief Frank Littlejohn quit and before James took over. Selvey was again chief when James quit and before Hord was hired. The charges against Hord were that he failed to investigate "bawdy houses," the Queen City Tourist Home and several other cases. When the indictments were dismissed, Hord was reinstated by council just before Christmas 1964 and he remained chief until 1966.

A key city official was to say more than a quarter century later that Hord "drew more brickbats than he deserved . . . but he might have been in a bit over his head." But another top city official of that era said years later that Hord was very independent and clashed from time to time with Veeder.

Later, John E. Ingersoll was Charlotte's police chief briefly before taking a federal job in 1968 and being replaced by John C. Goodman. Councilman Thrower, one of whose major interests was the police department, was against Ingersoll from the start because Ingersoll originally had been one of several asked to recommend a successor to Hord. Thrower said that when Ingersoll visited him at his business office before the council decision was to be made, Ingersoll let Thrower know that "I already have six votes on council." Thrower said he answered, "Well, you don't have seven." Thrower predicted that Ingersoll would not last two years and he proved to be an accurate prophet on that score. Thrower also said he was against Ingersoll's appointment because he had been handpicked by Veeder and the selection of the chief was supposed to be a council prerogative.

Former Councilman Short said he recalls Ingersoll observing that the city needed to find some "street-smart" policemen and not rely on those "who could read a book and pass an exam. He was questioning the way the personnel and police departments hired policemen, but it dawned on me that he was right . . . So getting blacks on the force was a good way to go, because they had some instincts and insights others who could just pass exams didn't have."

Former Assistant City Manager Carstarphen said he thought Ingersoll turned "an average police department into a much more professional one."

When it came time to replace Ingersoll, Councilman James Stegall, who had a private investigation firm, wanted the job. But he was opposed by Brookshire and Councilman Alexander, who said to friends that Stegall would "be a disaster from a race relations standpoint." Stegall lined up some votes on council, but not enough and Goodman was appointed. One newsman said years later that he thought Stegall would have attained sufficient votes to be appointed had not the news media alerted the public to Stegall's tactics. "Public pressure then killed his chances," the newsman said in 1993. Others gave the majority of the credit to Alexander. Carstarphen observed during his interview for this book that Goodman eased some of the tensions within the department that had developed under Ingersoll and said Goodman "could go both ways . . . as a modern police officer and a good old boy."

∞

Early in Brookshire's administration, Charlotte got its first full-time city attorney in John Morrisey. Morrisey attempted to be more proactive than his predecessors, who had been part-time city employees. His goal was to practice "preventive law." Years later, he recalled that he was approached by Whittington, who said he and his council colleagues were getting a lot of calls from lawyers asking to get title work from the city. Morrisey had been working from a short list of his own. Morrisey told Whittington to have each councilman give him (Morrisey) names of those who called them. "As long as they were capable and up to the city's standards, I said I'd use them. So we set up a rotating system. It worked out and was just part of politics," Morrisey said.

Thrower said that Morrisey knew more about municipal law than anyone in the state and was "a joy to work with." Bryant said he was never close to Morrisey, but found him "up-to-date and very competent."

∞

Herman Hoose, the city's traffic expert, was easily the city's best known and most colorful bureaucrat. "I liked every thing he did," said Bryant. "He was fearless, innovative and had a marvelous sense of humor."

"He was a wild man," recalled Carstarphen years later. "He was a great personality and character. He had big fights with merchants and neighborhoods. I think council wanted to get rid of him from time to time."

∞

Brookshire believed that Washington, more than Raleigh, was the place to seek federal funds. Charlotte-Mecklenburg was still tagged "the great state of Mecklenburg" by many of the state legislators and the city got little financial help from the General Assembly except for schools and health needs. Brookshire named local political power Paul Younts to head an intergovernmental task force to "gain maximum benefits from state and federal programs" in August 1965. Brookshire pointed out he was merely seeking to recover "our tax money." Bryant remembered that Brookshire argued the matter with him from time to time. "The money is there. If we don't get it, someone else will," Brookshire told Bryant, who, as a staunch conservative, hoped that enough cities would refuse federal funds so that Congress would take a totally new look at federal programs.

Carstarphen was the city's staff man for seeking federal grants. He recalled that Brookshire's firm determination to do something about Charlotte's slums was reinforced when, at a ceremony to launch an urban renewal program, a slum house almost collapsed on the mayor as he swung a sledgehammer.

Carstarphen said years later that Brookshire moved the city away from its traditional role of merely "picking up garbage and putting out fires" into new areas despite the fact that Brookshire was "basically a conservative man, but he was committed to making it a better city for everyone."

∞

As early as January 1963, Brookshire was calling for joint meetings of City Council and the County Commission. And the council tried taking the government to the people by holding a series of six council meetings in selected neighborhoods in 1968.

∞

Brookshire's files at UNC Charlotte contain a letter from Brookshire to author-editor Harry Golden thanking Golden for helping with a speech to be given in High Point. But he usually wrote his own speeches on yellow legal pads and then asked for input from key city staff members.

Chapter Three

How Segregated Was Charlotte?

The first sit-in demonstrations in Charlotte, led by 200 Johnson C. Smith University students, came in February 1960 and were directed against eight segregated downtown lunch counters. Charles Jones, one of the leaders, employed the technique used in Greensboro a week earlier. Dr. Reginald Hawkins, a local black dentist and ordained minister, was very involved in civil rights issues then as he was for many years afterward. Rather than desegregate, the lunch counters were closed. After months of negotiations, all of the stores except Sears, Roebuck desegregated their lunch counters July 8, 1960. Sears did desegregate soon after as did Woolworth's at Park Road and Amity Gardens shopping centers. The airport and bus station restaurants likewise were desegregated. Charlotte, following Winston-Salem, was the second city to take that step in North Carolina.

∞

Causing some concern at the time but without long-range major repercussions was a two-day rock-throwing incident involving Johnson C. Smith students in early 1961.

∞

Racial segregation ended at Belk Brothers' basement cafeteria and J.B. Ivey and Company's Tulip Terrace Restaurant in early December 1961 after two days of picketing by Johnson C. Smith University students led by divinity student Clyde Carter and Hawkins. Belk's mezzanine lunch counter and Ivey's basement lunch counter had been among the facilities desegregated 18 months before.

Hawkins, who was a staunch Democrat, clashed with Kelly Alexander Sr., state NAACP president, who was pushing for a two-party system. "If the Democrats don't give us what we want, we'll go where we can get it," Alexander was quoted as saying. In her 1976 master's thesis, D'Etta Leach wrote that Dr. Nathaniel Tross had been white Charlotte's favorite Negro leader, because he relied only on persuasion. Alexander used persuasion and the courts. Hawkins was not popular among whites because he used persuasion, then the courts and then, unlike the other two, demonstrations. Hawkins was accused and then indicted on charges of illegal registration of voters in April 1964. After years of legal wrangling, he achieved at least partial vindication in 1968 when the charges were dropped.

∞

Members of a dance troupe from India were refused service at a Charlotte restaurant in October 1961, and in November 1961 singer Mahalia Jackson had to stay in a private home during a Charlotte concert because the major hotels would not accept her. These incidents drew apologies from evangelist Billy Graham and Dr. John R. Cunningham, chairman of the Mayor's Committee on Human Relations. This led local black leaders to ask, "But who will apologize to us?"

∞

Brookshire had reorganized the dormant Friendly Relations Committee into the 27-member Mayor's Committee on Human Relations in July 1961 with Cunningham, former president of Davidson College, as chairman. Mayor James Smith, Brookshire's predecessor, had organized the Friendly Relations Committee the year before by mentioning "bombing incidents at Jewish houses of worship" and expressing regret that the committee had not been named prior to "the lunch counter demonstrations, which have recently occurred. You may be assured that the committee's first order of business will be to study this situation and make recommendations leading to a satisfactory settlement." In his statement announcing the new committee, Smith said "much progress" had occurred in the area of race relations, but there also was "a growing impatience among our Negro citizens to have equal consideration faster than our pattern of progress has permitted in the past." He added that the demonstrations, although non-violent, "do set up tensions and create ill will, which retard progress."

Brookshire said that when he established his committee he named Negroes who were "militant, but not extreme." Three years later, in a book on racial progress in the state, he wrote that "The Negro members were militant, but reasonable and were carefully selected for their leadership qualities." Extremists were left off the committee as Brookshire explained that he "did not wish the committee to be bargaining among its own members." Compared with black leaders in much of the rest of the nation, Brookshire's nominees were not even militant, just activists. But one political leader, who knew and knows Charlotte's African-American community as well as any white man, suggested that Charlotte never has had the black militancy that Durham and Winston-Salem had and that Brookshire did as well as he could, short of naming Hawkins, whom he couldn't abide, or college students. This same person said Fred Alexander, who later was to draw criticism from some segments within the black community for being an Uncle Tom, "said some of the most bitter things about white folks I've ever heard from a black man." Former *Charlotte Observer* reporter Susan Jetton agreed. Jetton, who covered Alexander while he was on the City Council and later in the State Senate, said she noted great bitterness in Alexander from time to time. But, she added, she believed he had learned the necessity of being cautious in order to survive politically. The obvious conclusion one draws after talking to those who knew him is that Alexander was a complex man—certainly not an Uncle Tom, yet also certainly not a militant leader in the mold of such younger men as Martin Luther King Jr. or even Andrew Young.

By 1969, the Mayor's Committee on Human Relations had become the Community Relations Committee which sought and obtained approval of federal funds to fight discrimination in employment. But the City Council voted not to receive the $14,000 grant and the project was abandoned. The county joined the city at about the same time to make it the Charlotte-Mecklenburg Community Relations Committee.

Kathleen "Kat" Crosby, who was active in educational, civil rights and other community issues throughout Brookshire's and Belk's administrations, praised Brookshire for reviving the committee. "Any white man in the 1960s who even *pretended* to do something progressive (in the racial field) was a hero," she said in 1993. "It was enough for him to have the guts to know to do something and to do it," she said.

She said Alexander was the most important black man

in Charlotte in the past century—for whites and blacks. Alexander "got behind the gate when we couldn't. And he was calm behind the gate and found out how the political process worked. But he took abuse and even blacks were jealous . . . And he knew he *really* wasn't inside the gate."

". . . He was a fierce fighter for blacks, but the news media rarely quoted him . . . I read some powerful statements (in speeches he made) against racism and injustice, but they were not covered in the media. He only became a hero after he died," Crosby said.

∞

Brookshire was named chairman of the statewide Mayor's Coordinating Committee, which in 1964 produced a book, *North Carolina and the Negro*, chronicling the experiences of 55 cities in dealing with "the organized revolt of Negroes against segregation."

In the Charlotte section of that book was the claim that "Racial discrimination has now been largely eliminated in the community life of Charlotte." The section went on to deal with progress in ending segregation in all walks of life and gave credit to the Chamber of Commerce and the Mayor's Committee on Human Relations.

∞

President Lyndon Johnson named Brookshire and Cunningham as advisors on implementing his new civil rights bill. Brookshire was only one of seven mayors on the panel. Brookshire had been offered the full-time job of director of the group, but that would have required him to move to Washington and he declined. Former Florida Governor LeRoy Collins took the job.

∞

Brookshire spoke out courageously on racial issues— particularly for a Southern businessman-mayor in the early

1960s. He called his program "Total Citizenship," and said the areas of his concern were job opportunities, slum clearance, hospital care, education and park facilities.

Harvey Gantt, who was to enter City Hall as a councilman under Mayor John Belk and then serve as mayor for two terms 14 years after Brookshire left, said in 1993 that he remembered Brookshire coming before the council to complain about the budget, which was escalating at a faster pace than the population. As far as Brookshire's contributions in the area of race relations, Gantt said that what was accepted as commonplace in the 1980s was "revolutionary in the 1960s" when Brookshire served.

Gantt recalled sitting in Brookshire's back yard on Huntington Park Drive and listening to Brookshire say that he believed his (Brookshire's) greatest contributions were in the field of race relations. Gantt said he then thought Brookshire was just saying that because Gantt was black. Later, he said, he came to know that Brookshire said the same thing to whomever asked, black or white. Brookshire as a businessman looked ahead to the negative impact racial unrest could have on Charlotte in the future, Gantt said.

∞

Jack Bullard was a Baptist minister in Raleigh when he was named executive director of the Community Relations Committee in March 1968 and was still in the position in 1994. Brookshire had been pushing the committee to hire a full-time director since mid-1967. Bullard said Brookshire "was a remarkable person to be able to go against his training and all his cultural background. He was much more impressive than a radical, who does not make much of a change." Bullard credited Brookshire's Christian faith in large measure for being behind his courageous stands on racial matters. "He got his practices in line with his teaching," Bullard said. But, Bullard noted, Brookshire also knew that a calm racial climate was good for business.

Years later, former Assistant City Manager Bill Carstarphen said Bullard "did a lot to bring Charlotte to understand what it had to deal with (in terms of race) . . . He was extremely effective and had a major impact on how Charlotte moved through the 1960s and early 1970s." Carstarphen said Bullard was shrewd in lining people up on his side without their realizing it until "it was too late to back out." He said that Veeder and Bullard often clashed and "he (Bullard) wanted me to work on Veeder." Carstarphen also said that Bullard was the first to see that the highly controversial Paul Jones was not working out as the director of the Model Cities program.

∞

Noting that one-third of Charlotte's population was Negro (that was the term used then), Brookshire urged seeking social justice by changing from "live and let live" to "live and help live." Regardless of "how we feel personally, we cannot escape our community responsibilities," he said. He told a Greensboro civic club in May 1963 that "the concept of freedom leaves out no man." Yet he also called on black citizens to be more patient and to accept the responsibilities of full and equal citizenship. He went before a regional NAACP group to say that demonstrations had "gone far enough."

Joe Epley, a former television newsman and later a public relations executive, said that Brookshire deserves credit for leading Charlotte through the "biggest social upheaval since the Civil War" and in doing so achieved national recognition for the city.

Brookshire, writing in his family history, said that the "most acute and agonizing problems facing my administration were in the area of race relations, confronted as we were throughout the South with vigorous demands of black citizens for equal rights and opportunities, often accompanied by threats. This brought on a social upheaval that had to be dealt with in terms of change in long-established social and economic patterns. This conflict was between black activists, who wanted all their demands met at once, and whites, many of whom were good substantial citizens who wanted no change at all from the status quo. The mayor's office was caught in the middle . . . That Charlotte acted with wisdom and courage in doing these things to keep civil peace and correct inequities of the past, and did them voluntarily before the 1964 Act of Congress required it, I think is credit to our community of Charlotte-Mecklenburg. I positively think that this voluntary action enabled us to avoid the violence of murder, riots, arson and looting, which plagued many of our cities."

But while hoping for the best, the city also planned for the worst. City officials quietly and privately worked on contingency plans should racial riots hit the city. The major focus of the plans was how the police would react in case of confrontations with demonstrators or rioters.

Sue Myrick, who served as mayor in 1987–91, said Brookshire will be best remembered for his work in human relations. "He really moved us as a city when no one else wanted to take steps for integration. Not only was he a spokesman, but he practiced what he preached . . . And he went out on a limb with his social set."

Brookshire's stand probably did not win him as much disfavor among the white socially elite as did Judge James McMillan's handling of the school desegregation situation, but he did lose some fair-weather friends. The difference may have been that McMillan was seen as interpreting the law, whereas Brookshire was seen as carrying out the law, unpopular though it was in certain circles.

∞

In December 1962 Brookshire was pushing another major theme—businesses should build in the Brooklyn redevelopment area. He also spoke often and forcefully on the matter of crime. He began his campaign in the spring of 1962 by arguing that race relations and crime were closely intertwined: "Low-income, underprivileged areas breed crime . . . Negroes as a race are hampered in self-development by economic and social pressures." He asked for a comprehensive report from United Community Services on the subject. Charlotte was not happy to learn in mid-1963 that crime had increased nearly 25 percent in the city during 1962. Brookshire resumed his anti-crime crusade in 1963 after hearing a policeman remark at a crime scene, in answer to a question, "It is only a murder."

∞

Events were pushing Charlotte and the South to a confrontation with the inevitability of change. Brookshire endorsed Governor Terry Sanford's call for an end to racial discrimination in January 1963. A tentative agreement to desegregate some hotels and motels during the International Trade Fair that spring did not hold up and the establishments reverted to enforcing the color barrier when the fair ended. In May 1963 Johnson C. Smith University students again marched downtown to protest segregation.

On Sunday, May 19, 1963, just after attending Sunday school and church at Myers Park Methodist Church, Brookshire called his friend J. Ed Burnside, who was the new president of the Charlotte Chamber of Commerce. The mayor suggested it was time to desegregate Charlotte's restaurants.

Coincidentally or not, Reginald Hawkins led students from Johnson C. Smith University on a march from the campus to the County Courthouse May 20.

Burnside gathered the chamber's executive committee together and Brookshire spoke to the issue, saying that not only was desegregating restaurants the right thing to do, it was the smart thing to do to avoid negative economic consequences. But the mayor stressed the moral obligations. The degrees of moral outrage, wise business acumen and paternalism on the part of the businessmen in the mixture has been and will be debated without agreement. Veteran television newscaster Doug Mayes said years later he thought the major influences on Brookshire were from the Methodist Church, which Mayes said is traditionally more tolerant of various views than some religions, and Brookshire's alma mater, Duke University, which, of course, is a Methodist institution. Because of what happened in Little Rock and Birmingham, there was no doubt that the businessmen feared the prospect of demonstrations by Negro leaders and students.

∞

Brookshire identified himself with Atlanta Mayor Ivan Allen Jr., who served as mayor of Atlanta in 1961–69. In a 1971 review of Allen's book on his administration, Jonathan Yardley, a 1961 graduate of UNC Chapel Hill, addressed the issues of motive:

" . . . For it is a book about growth and benefits, and about adjusting positively to racial demands, it is also a book about the risks growth entails and about the business establishment's approach to racial matters . . . Other Southern cities, most notably our friends in Charlotte, have been busily attempting to follow the Atlanta model, believing it to be the ideal city of the future . . . Mr. Allen is a nearly classic instance of the contemporary version of the Southern patrician . . . It is entirely true that much of the South's racial progress is traceable to men like Ivan Allen: 'Whether we were sincerely liberal is inconsequential. We succeeded in Atlanta because we were realistic . . . It is wonderful to be idealistic and to speak about human values, but you are not going to be able to do one thing about them if you are not economically strong.'"

We'll never know if Stan Brookshire would have endorsed the totality of Allen's remarks or agreed with Yardley's assessment, but it's a good bet he would have.

∞

The chamber's executive committee approved a resolution on the desegregation of businesses written by C.A. "Pete" McKnight of *The Charlotte Observer* and passed it on to the full chamber board, which also agreed—despite the fact that the chamber still had no Negro directors. The resolution said the chamber directors "recommended that all businesses in this community catering to the general public be opened immediately to all customers without regard to race, creed or color." Burnside told the news media that the chamber did not want to tell "any man what to do or what not to do. We only wish to state what we think is the right principle." Brookshire said he believed the "total city will follow this leadership."

∞

Reached in Tallahassee in 1993, Charles C. Crawford, who was vice president (the top staff position) of the chamber in the early 1960s, said he didn't remember who was the Charlotte Chamber's first black member or how the desegregation process of the chamber itself was accomplished. Crawford said the action was so smooth, it simply wasn't a major thing.

Randy Penninger, who did his master's thesis on the late Fred Alexander, produced a clipping from *The Charlotte Post,* dated February 24, 1962, that said Alexander became the first Negro chamber member February 6, 1962. White businessman C.D. Spangler Sr. had said as early as the first meeting of the Mayor's Committee on Human Relations in August 1961 that the chamber should open its membership to black businessmen. Alexander told writer Pat Watters in 1964 that desegregation occurred after the chamber leadership realized it would be futile to attempt to get U.S. Secretary of State Dean Rusk to speak to the chamber's annual dinner if the chamber were still segregated. Alexander said the black chamber members, who would be attending their first annual chamber meeting, were told that they would be seated with whites who supported the cause and would be friendly.

∞

At the suggestion of James "Slug" Claiborne, then only 27 years old, the white businessmen agreed to team up with their black counterparts to integrate Charlotte restaurants. Abel Girault, who managed the Manger Motor Inn, agreed to be first on May 29, 1963. The first team consisted of Brookshire; Dr. John Cunningham; Alexander; and Dr. Moses Belton, public relations director at Johnson C. Smith. The news media had promised not to publicize the effort until after it was tried. Partial details were made public at a 4 p.m. news conference Wednesday, May 29, but the names of the establishments were not announced until May 31. The first restaurants involved were located in the Manger Inn, Heart of Charlotte Motel, Downtowner Inn, Queen Charlotte Hotel and Barringer Hotel.

Claiborne convinced 14 other restaurants to participate and this part of the desegregation plan was accomplished two days later. Claiborne said in 1993 that the major problem was finding enough blacks to accompany the white businessmen. It was also noted that the city's Greek restaurant owners balked at participating initially and were late in dropping the color barriers at their establishments. Ralph Stern, vice president of Southern Knitwear Mills, pushed the Greek restaurants to move through a series of letters to Greek restaurant owners.

∞

The Atlanta Chamber of Commerce recommended to its members desegregation of their facilities this same week.

∞

The Reverend Martin Luther King Jr. spoke to six black high school senior classes at the Charlotte Coliseum May 30, 1963. He stayed at the Manger Motor Inn, "a plush downtown motel," according to my story in *The Charlotte News*. I quoted King as praising Charlotte "for meaningful and significant strides in race relations. I'd like to publicly commend those persons working in such an enlightened way to make progress a reality. Other communities and chambers of commerce in the South can learn from Charlotte. What is done here may well save many sections in our beloved South from dark nights of tension and racial violence." King challenged the students to be ready for "the winds of change that are blowing, sweeping away the old order and bringing into being a new order with new challenges and new responsibilities." He drew wide applause when he said, "We realize that black is as dangerous as white supremacy . . . God is interested in the freedom of the whole human race."

Dr. Reginald Hawkins later was to tell writer Pat Watters that he had pushed the chamber to act with his threats of protests, even the threat of bringing King back to town. Yet

Burnside told Watters that the chamber action was "moral, not economic."

Actually, before this and even before King had stayed at the Manger Inn, the color barrier had fallen with no public notice! The previous August, former Wake Forest coach Paul Amen, then a Charlotte bank executive, told Claiborne he had put together a pre-season exhibition between the Washington Redskins and the Philadelphia Eagles. Both teams had black players. The Manger agreed to take the Redskins and Dwight Phillips agreed to lodge the Eagles at his Coliseum Inn, but no restaurant in that area would agree to feed the team. Claiborne said he'd feed them at his Barclay's Cafeteria and did so. And an integrated Temple University basketball team stayed at a Charlotte hotel in 1958.

∞

Although the Visulite Theatre on Elizabeth Avenue had already desegregated, the barriers at the other theaters took more time and patience. Claiborne nevertheless remembers this part of the desegregation process as being orderly. The plan was for couples from the Johnson C. Smith student body to purchase tickets at previously all-white theaters and sit in designated areas once inside. It was only by appointment and reservation by name. Behind each couple was a plainclothes policemen. "We saw a lot of terrible movies," one black person involved in the project later told Watters.

Black leaders did not see progress as positively as did whites. When civil rights lawyer Julius Chambers came to Charlotte in 1964, he saw segregation still as the order of the day. Chambers told *The Charlotte Observer* in 1988 that he eventually began to see Charlotte change and he also began to feel pride in what the city had accomplished, albeit slowly. When he first came to Charlotte, however—he told the *Observer's* Frye Gaillard years later—"I thought Charlotte in the 1960s was almost like the South Africa I visited 20 years later."

∞

Attorney General Robert Kennedy wrote Brookshire to say how he was "impressed by the striking progress, which has been made in Charlotte."

∞

In November 1965 Charlotte was outraged by the middle-of-the-night bombing of the homes of four well-known black leaders—Kelly Alexander, Fred Alexander, Julius Chambers and Reginald Hawkins. Although no one was injured, the homes were damaged, particularly the Alexanders' homes where the bombs were placed on the front steps. The other bombs apparently were thrown from passing cars. Brookshire condemned the act and a "Rally of Apology" was held at Ovens Auditorium with Dr. Roy L. Wilkins, executive secretary of the NAACP, as the main speaker. Brookshire said at the rally that "together we can and will win the battle against hate and prejudice. We will not be deterred." Years later, former Mayor Gantt said he had been greatly impressed as a young man that Brookshire and other white leaders were on the stage at Ovens Auditorium lending their support to the event.

Kat Crosby, who spoke at the meeting, said in 1993 that the Ku Klux Klan delivered a written threat to her home just before the meeting. She called the FBI and handed over the letter to the agency. Other speakers received similar threats, but Crosby said she wasn't really worried because she knew even the KKK wouldn't dare to bomb Ovens with so many important white people there.

As he left office, Brookshire said the bombings were the low point in his time in office. *The Charlotte Observer* started a fund to pay for the damages done to the four homes. The identity of the terrorists was never discovered, even though local police, state troopers, the SBI and the FBI investigated. Although the Ku Klux Klan never claimed credit, nor was there any proof of its involvement, it was widely thought that Klansmen were behind the incident, D'Etta Leach wrote in her 1976 master's thesis. Someone who had been close to Fred Alexander during that time said Alexander always believed a specific white politician had been behind the bombings.

∞

But prejudice and discrimination remained deeply rooted in all aspects of society. Brookshire was obviously the leader among white elected officials in Charlotte, perhaps the state, but he still found himself pressured.

Legal action by 41 Negro students and parents threatened to cancel the 1965 Shrine Bowl game because no black players were picked on either team. The protesters asked the City Parks and Recreation Department to not allow the game to go on in its Memorial Stadium. Jimmy Kirkpatrick, a brilliant Myers Park High School halfback, had thrilled crowds in scoring 14 touchdowns his senior year, but two other Myers Park players, both white, had been picked to represent the Mustangs in the December 4 game. Brookshire and others intervened and the game went on as scheduled, thanks to a court order. Black players participated the following year.

∞

In late 1965, Brookshire defended city government against criticism in the media for lack of action against blockbusting, dealing with transitional neighborhoods (Fourth Ward was cited as an example) and creeping blight. Brookshire answered the criticism by saying blockbusting (using scare tactics to get homeowners to sell) was something the city could deal with, but the matter of transitional neighborhoods was more an issue of personal choice. At the request of realtor T.R. Lawing, City Council in November 1965 approved an anti-blockbusting ordinance, which was found unconstitutional by Superior Court Judge Frank Snepp in October 1967. *The Charlotte Observer* reported cases of blockbusting as late as October 1968.

∞

Amazingly little was made of it in news reports at the time, but a cross was burned on Brookshire's lawn August 26, 1966. The mayor discovered the remains of the cross burning when he went out to pick up *The Charlotte Observer* in the morning. He discarded the remains and reseeded the spot immediately so that his wife Edith would not know of it and be fearful. Police were assigned to keep a watch on the area for the next several weeks and when Mrs. Brookshire asked about that, the mayor made light of it. Eventually he did tell his wife, but only after he was sure the danger was past and it would not alarm her. Brookshire also received threats and vulgar comments in the mail and on the telephone throughout his tenure in office.

∞

Human resources consultant James Ross recalls Brookshire with great admiration. "He was the epitome of a Southern gentleman," Ross said when interviewed for this book.

Ross particularly recalled one incident in late 1967 or early 1968. Brookshire couldn't understand why anyone, including young blacks, were not as enthusiastic as he about Charlotte and the opportunities the city offered. (His successor John Belk felt the same way—probably even more so.) A meeting was set up at City Hall between Brookshire and two "angry young men," Ross and Frederick Douglass Ford, who worked for James K. Polk at the Charlotte Bureau on Employment, Training and Placement.

Ross remembered that Brookshire opened the meeting by talking about what his administration had done in the areas of civil rights. But when the mayor said that "as long as you are 'qualified,' you can get work," the two young black men interrupted to say that white people often interpreted "qualified" in ways to exclude blacks. They cited examples to prove their case. Brookshire was "taken aback" by their vehemence, Ross said.

Yet Brookshire never blinked or backed down during the two-hour meeting even when Ross and Ford became "aggressive and assertive." They felt the meeting had been a success because Brookshire promised not to tolerate "artificial barriers" and was instrumental in implementing a wide-ranging summer jobs program soon after. Ross said that when one department head balked at participating, City Manager Veeder made it clear that the recalcitrant city official would be involved no matter what his private feelings were.

Brookshire, Ross recalled, "gave me one of the highest compliments I ever got when he called me a 'responsible militant.' But I worried about my reputation on the streets after he said that."

Ross gave Brookshire, Veeder and Police Chief John Ingersoll high marks for their performances in the areas of civil rights. "You could go to them with any reasonable request and you'd be heard and something would get done," he said. Brookshire subsequently named Ross to serve on his Community Relations Committee.

∞

The Charlotte Area Fund had been created in August

1963 after Paul Ylvisaker of the Ford Foundation had challenged a United Community Services gathering earlier in the year to fight the roots of poverty, rather than simply to treat the symptoms. Governor Sanford got a major jump on the federal anti-poverty programs when he established the North Carolina Fund. The Charlotte Area Fund was approved for a comprehensive project in April 1964. When the federal Office of Economic Development was established, Charlotte set up such programs as Head Start, Adult Education, Family and Children's Services, Legal Aid, Project New Careers, Neighborhood Corps, Concentrated Employment Program and three neighborhood centers.

By the fall of 1968, lawyer Mark Bernstein issued a report designed to correct problems that had arisen. Bernstein's report said that the Charlotte Area Fund board, which had been headed by fellow lawyer William Mulliss, had abdicated its responsibilities to the staff, according to media reports of the time.

∞

After Martin Luther King was killed in Memphis in April 1968, Brookshire declared an official day of mourning and he and County Commission Chairman Jim Martin imposed a 9 p.m.–5 a.m. curfew across the city and county. Brookshire warned that violence would not be tolerated. The curfew was successfully enforced for four days.

Brookshire later said Charlotte escaped the riots, lootings and burnings that hit other cities because of such diverse things as continuing dialogue with blacks; strong bi-racial leadership; federal programs such as Model Cities and Equal Opportunity; the police department's community relations program; an absence of young black militants; Johnson C. Smith's students being on vacation; the curfew that was imposed and respected; and the fact that black political candidates in Charlotte discouraged violence in order not to damage their own political positions and chances.

Gantt observed in 1993 that he believed "Fred Alexander kept the lid on racial tension in the black community." Alexander, Gantt said, saw Brookshire as a patrician businessman who began to push for progress for blacks. The "coalition of power" of Southeast Charlotte and the black community was detrimental, however, to other groups, such as poor whites, Gantt said. This coalition, therefore, was good and bad. Alexander was a near czar, he said, and some said racial issues were suppressed. "I don't know how it will ultimately be measured," he said. Another result of Alexander's control was that Johnson C. Smith University never became the focal point of the civil rights struggle here as did black colleges in other Tar Heel cities.

∞

Former City Manager Veeder many years later recalled a humorous incident from 1968. Because of the threat of racial trouble, police in riot gear were stationed at The Square in downtown Charlotte just after the assassination of Martin Luther King Jr. Veeder, along with the police and young blacks, were milling around the area. Veeder said he spotted a huge white policeman, perhaps 6 feet 6 inches tall, nearby. He then saw a young black man approach the massive policeman and quip, "Remember, if trouble starts, you're disqualified!"

∞

On a more serious note, Veeder said that Brookshire and Bullard worked very diligently in this period to diffuse any problems that might occur and that Brookshire's efforts in the past on race relations paid off in 1968. Former City Councilman Don Bryant reported that Veeder also deserved a large measure of credit for keeping down racial conflict in the 1960s. Bryant said that Veeder at least once heard reports of potential racial unrest and canceled a two-week vacation to stay in Charlotte to walk the streets to try to convince young blacks that Charlotte city government was at least trying to achieve progress for all its citizens. Bryant said Veeder made no public mention of his efforts and he found out about it only much later.

∞

Brookshire did not approve of the Southern Christian Leadership Conference's Poor People's March coming through Charlotte in mid-1968.

∞

When Charlotte was considering a public accommodations ordinance in 1968, City Attorney Henry Underhill got a call to come to Brookshire's home. Upon arriving there, Underhill found several city councilmen as well as two white barbers. The barbers showed great anxiety, Underhill recalled years later, because they feared the ordinance might require them to cut black people's hair—which they didn't feel they had the skill to do. Underhill said he noted no prejudice, just lack of confidence.

The ordinance had "only a fragile majority on council," Underhill recalled, so he altered the proposed ordinance to exclude businesses who offer services for which they had no specific training. The ordinance passed easily.

Brookshire endorsed a local anti-discrimination ordinance on employment, but said there was no need for a local open housing ordinance. The employment ordinance eventually passed. He did say that consideration should be given to a local gun ordinance, even though a statewide statute would be a better approach.

∞

The issue of removing a fence between racially segregated Elmwood and Pinewood cemeteries lost 4-3 on four occasions, so Councilman Alexander waited until one of the opponents was absent from a council meeting, reintroduced the issue, and drew a 3-3 tie vote. Brookshire broke the tie and another racial barrier of the past came down.

∞

In September of 1968 Brookshire named a task force "to develop greater economic opportunities for the Negro in the business field" while working with the Small Business Administration. Contractor C. D. Spangler Sr. and banker Walter Tucker were among those named to the committee.

∞

By 1968, 24 of 390 policemen and 751 of 2,651 city employees were black. The city had had black policemen for 25 years, but only in the late 1960s were they assigned as anything but patrolmen.

In the private sector, 1964 saw the first black teller hired by a white-owned bank, Wachovia, under the leadership of Scott Cramer.

∞

Dr. W. L. Anderson Jr., assistant school superintendent for personnel, wrote Brookshire in September 1968 to urge the mayor to act more forcefully to open white neighborhoods to blacks. The real estate community was not assuming a leadership role, Anderson said. Anderson said the segregated situation as it existed stymied the hiring of teachers and caused long drives by some black teachers. Brookshire responded by saying that people tended to live with people "of common interests" and that lots of people had long rides to work. Hidden Valley at the time was the focus of tension as it evolved from a predominantly white to a predominantly black neighborhood. Brookshire was known to have spoken privately against integration of housing, yet when his Community Relations Committee began pursing the matter, he did not interfere. Committee member Howard Arbuckle advised the group that the local public accommodations law could be used to push integrated housing unless "some judge says no." CRC Executive Director Jack Bullard said the real estate community reacted positively to the committee's work in 1968. The Community Relations Committee won its first housing bias case in September 1968—when a black teacher at Independence High School rented an apartment from which he previously had been turned away.

∞

Brookshire was still a man of his times, for in 1990, near the end of his life, Brookshire wrote a letter to *The Charlotte Observer* to complain of the paper's "continued assault" on private clubs.

"Private clubs in no way fit the category of public accommodations and in no way impinge individual or group rights. I see nothing un-Christian, unethical, immoral or illegal when citizens of similar interests personally finance the facilities and operation of a private venture that provides them with the activities and amenities in which they have an interest . . . Membership in a private club is a privilege, not a right." And although that position was and is held by many Charlotte citizens, including at least one member of Brookshire's City Council and by at least one member of a City Council of the 1980s, it stood in contrast to the amazingly forward-thinking, courageous and positive stands taken by Brookshire in the 1960s.

Mayor Stan Brookshire's 1961–65 City Council: John Thrower, Steve Dellinger, Gibson Smith, Jim Whittington, Brookshire, Claude Albea, Don Bryant, Sandy Jordan.

1970 Charlotte News *Man of the Year Luncheon—*Seated left to right: *Colonel Norman Pease, Oliver Rowe, J. Ed Burnside, Stan Brookshire, Carl McCraw, Herbert Bridges.* Standing left to right: *C.W. "Pat" Gilchrist, James Cannon, John Stickley, W.T. Harris, James Harris, John Belk, Tom Belk, Zeb Strawn, Jack Erwin, George Broadrick.*

Mayor Brookshire with Roy Wilkins, executive secretary of the NAACP, on his right, and Kelly Alexander, president of the North Carolina NAACP, on his left at the November 28, 1965, rally in protest of bombings.

Top: *Mayor and Mrs. Brookshire with Dr. Billy Graham at the 1962 Peru Crusade.*

Bottom: *Bill Veeder addresses former City Councilman Brevard Myers, former Mayor Brookshire, former Councilmen Gibson Smith, Herbert Hitch and Don Bryant at a ceremony marking Veeder's retirement January 4, 1974.*

Top: *Brooklyn as it appeared in the early 1960s.*

Bottom: *This Brooklyn house almost fell on Mayor Brookshire when he swung a sledgehammer as he launched the urban renewal program in 1961.*

The recently completed Wachovia Building dominates downtown Charlotte in the mid-1970s.

Aerial shot of Charlotte taken by Jeep Hunter of The Charlotte News *from a blimp in October 1964.*

Charlotte's airport through the Brookshire and Belk years as it appeared from the parking lot.

Mayor Stanford R. Brookshire

Chapter Four

Rebuilding the Downtown Area

As the city's director of urban renewal, Vernon Sawyer in January 1959 began the process leading to the slum clearance and redevelopment of 238 acres (later increased) of Brooklyn in Charlotte's Second Ward in the proverbial shadow of the downtown office towers. Sawyer was to fight the sometimes unpopular battle on behalf of the city for 26 years. Marshall Park, the Education Center, a new First Baptist Church, the Government Plaza, and the ramps and freeways leading to I-77 would replace Friendship Baptist, the House of Prayer for All People, Second Ward School, Myers Street Elementary School, and the homes of many black Charlotteans. The $10-million, 10-year program eventually cleared 263 acres of commercial and residential blight. More than 1,000 families and another nearly 400 individuals were relocated along with more than 215 businesses. The federal government paid two-thirds of the cost and the city the remainder. Brooklyn was bounded by East Third and East Fourth, Sugar Creek, the rear of Morehead Street lots and the Southern Railway and South Brevard.

Brookshire was to write later in his family history:

"When, under this grant-in-aid plan, we launched the Brooklyn slum clearance program to clear 238 acres of disgraceful, crime- and disease-ridden slums in the shadow of the uptown office buildings in 1961, there were loud public protests. Many property owners objected and businessmen objected on the grounds that it was not ethically or morally right to condemn and acquire property (except for public purposes) under the rights of eminent domain, and then sell it for private development. Another argument was that we should not take federal money and subject ourselves to the dictates (guidelines) from Washington. The opposition overlooked two valid points: (1) that acquisition was possible only under the rights of eminent domain (absentee and other slum owners did not want to sell), and (2) the federal money is our tax money allocated by Congress for this program and if we did not take our share of it, it would go to other cities."

Because the program was what Brookshire called "innovative and unpopular," the voters were not asked to approve bonds for the city's share, but Charlotte undertook the program in five phases over 10 years and used ad valorem taxes to pay for it.

∞

Brookshire complained in his first term that the city was 15 to 20 years behind in planning and programming. He also said that had the city had a housing code years before, fewer slums would exist. And had urban renewal (which all members of Brookshire's city councils except Don Bryant generally approved of) been in existence 15 years before, the city would have a YMCA, YWCA, Red Cross building, coliseum and auditorium in the downtown area. Instead, the YWCA and Red Cross built new facilities on Park Road.

A new housing code aimed at preventing slums was passed and in place in Brookshire's first term.

As stated, Brookshire got general support for urban renewal from members of the city councils elected during his eight years in office—except for Bryant, who said that while he "abhorred the slums of Brooklyn," he hated the idea of eminent domain even more. Bryant's approach was to tax the slum land at its highest and best use, thereby forcing the landowners to remove the slum buildings and convert the land to business uses. "It would have been more ragged than planning everything at one time," Bryant admitted years later. He said he also knew that it wasn't a matter of ridding the city of slums, but merely moving them elsewhere. When someone suggested in 1964 that urban renewal would be more popular under another name, Bryant good-naturedly remarked that he'd be against it even if urban renewal were named for him.

One early but crucial vote in 1960 on the Brooklyn project did only pass by a 5-2 or 4-3 vote (depending on what report you accept) and that occurred only when Councilman Gibson Smith switched his vote to the affirmative.

John Morrisey, who served as city attorney in 1961–65, said years later that the greatest satisfaction he got from his years in Charlotte came from assisting in the clearing of the Brooklyn slums. When interviewed at his daughter's house in Charlotte in early 1993, Morrisey said he recalled walking in Brooklyn and seeing open sewers running through the area with children playing near them. "I couldn't believe it (how bad it was) and that says nothing about the houses. I took my grandchildren to Marshall Park the other day and saw how beautiful it was. That was enough pay-off (for the years spent in City Hall)," Morrisey said.

Brookshire constantly pushed for speeding up urban renewal. In September 1961, the new mayor said action on the second phase of the five-part slum clearance plan for Brooklyn should begin. The city had been ready to move on the second phase six months after the first phase was approved in June 1961, but approval didn't come until three-and-a-half years later as the city moved to construct Earle Village and Edwin Towers. The first section of 36 acres was bounded by East Third, South Brevard, South Davidson and Independence Boulevard. The second phase, begun in 1964, was bounded by East Fourth, South Davidson, South McDowell and Independence Boulevard. More than 475 families lived within the second phase. The third phase began in early 1965 and the fourth phase in June 1966. The fourth phase included 40 acres bounded by Independence Boulevard, Ridge Street, Kenilworth and South McDowell. The infamous Blue Heaven area, generally considered by many white Charlotteans as the worst of the city's slum pockets as far as physical conditions and crime were concerned, was within this area. The fifth phase was approved in June 1969 just after Brookshire left office and was completed in June 1977, just before Brookshire's successor, John Belk, left office. That section was used primarily for the widening of Independence Boulevard and interchanges.

Sawyer said in 1980 that the land in Brooklyn, which was worth $2.9 million in 1959, was then valued at $29 million. Nearly $9 million in federal money had gone into the Brooklyn project. Clearing began in December 1961 when Brookshire swung a sledgehammer at a house that almost collapsed on him. The last sale of land cleared in the Brooklyn project was sold in 1976 to Washburn Graphics for its headquarters at McDowell and Baxter.

Zeb C. Strawn, president of Citizens Bank of Charlotte, was named chairman of the Citizens Advisory Committee on Urban Redevelopment in June 1962. He replaced Harry G. Brown, president of the Board of Realtors, who had been ineffectual, according to news reports at the time. The Citizens Committee on Urban Redevelopment, appointed by Mayor James Smith in the late 1950s, had met only three times—all in 1959—by the time Brookshire was elected in the spring of 1961.

In October 1962 the eradication of the Brooklyn slums was stymied by the lack of suitable, decent and affordable replacement housing. Brookshire said the private sector couldn't afford to provide the housing and federal programs were essential.

He added:

"Before we brand public housing as socialism, let us consider that it is no closer to socialism than county homes, welfare programs, social security or our United Appeal. All have in common a humanitarian interest in helping those who need help. You can add to that our interest in building a better, as well as a bigger, city."

Brookshire and other city leaders saw that not only were the slums unsightly, they restricted the growth of the downtown area. Third Street needed to be widened and the Northwest Expressway needed to be built and these could not be accomplished unless Brooklyn was cleared. The city needed growing room and Brooklyn also lay between the downtown and the rapidly developing medical facilities at Kings and Morehead. Railway tracks split the downtown area. Particularly troublesome to city leaders were the tracks from East Trade to East Second, between College and Brevard streets.

In late 1966, the city was spending $300,000 on the

Brooklyn redevelopment project on a pay-as-you-go basis. The city also decided to use $5.5 million of bond money to redevelop Dilworth, Greenville (along Statesville Avenue just north of the downtown area), First Ward and portions of the downtown area. The Inter-governmental Task Force, headed by Paul Younts, had recommended this course. The 23 acres in Dilworth that were involved in the 1969–70 project were bounded by South Boulevard, Rensselaer, Euclid and Templeton. Nearly 100 families and another 40 individuals along with 16 businesses were relocated. Constructed were 116 high-rise apartments and 122 cottages in Strawn Village.

The city's 1960 general development plan had called for preservation of Fourth Ward, but that didn't really start until 15 years later when the Junior League, with help from Knight Publishing Company, Exxon Corporation and Ivey's, refurbished the old Berryhill House.

∞

Brookshire in May 1962 reported that the $3.5 million westside grade-separation project had been launched with $600,000 from Governor Terry Sanford and co-operation from Southern Railway. Access to the downtown area was restricted because autos often had to wait for trains to pass. Warehouses lined the spur line along College Street. The old passenger terminal on Graham Street was to be removed also. By the end of 1963, the grade-separation project was 50 percent completed and the city had begun acquiring right-of-way for the Northwest Expressway. Two hundred parcels had been acquired by late 1964. The grade-separation project was completed by December 1964 at a cost about $200,000 under the original estimates. The project involved building a 1.4-mile-long mound to raise the railroad tracks to make room for five streets to pass underneath. New underpasses were to be built at Morehead, Fourth, Trade, Fifth and Sixth streets. One spur track remained at Fifth Street, but only one or two box cars moved over the track each month.

∞

On another issue that would reappear throughout the next several decades, Brookshire, near the end of his eight years in office, had to defend the city's record on the westside. Even into the 1990s, westside residents were complaining about inequities.

∞

The city had 1,420 public housing units at four sites in late 1962. Six hundred new public housing units were approved by council by the end of 1963. Thirty acres of land were acquired for what would become Edwin Towers and Earle Village. Three thousand housing units were brought up to standard in 1963 and 700 units were demolished. The following year saw 4,100 units brought up to standard and 650 units demolished.

Between the spring of 1962 and November 1965, 9,905 dwellings were raised to acceptable standards. Another 2,213 were demolished under the housing code, 485 under urban renewal, 393 under expressway programs, and 360 to build 600 public housing units. Brookshire was in the forefront in pushing for progress on all these fronts.

Yet in his 1969 book, *The South and the Nation*, Atlanta author Pat Watters wrote that Southern cities, including Atlanta, New Orleans and Charlotte, demolished homes at a faster pace than they built new housing. "In Charlotte, an average of 1,100 housing units were demolished each year from 1965 to 1968, and were replaced by only 425 public housing units during the same period. And so on, across the South," Watters wrote.

∞

Brookshire warned in early 1964 that downtown real estate values were declining. He pointed out the need to improve Third, Fourth, Fifth, Sixth, 28th, Brevard and Caldwell Streets and said the city should bury unsightly downtown utility wires. In April 1965, Brookshire proposed stripping out 14 blocks of railroad tracks east of the Square. The priorities remained East Trade to East Second and between College and Brevard. By 1967, five underpasses were in place in the uptown area.

∞

The 1965 bond issue of $21.1 million went to improve portions of East Third, West Third, West Fourth, East Fifth, Sixth, the Mint-Pine connector and Poplar, as well as expressways, water and sewer facilities, a police building and fire station.

∞

But Brookshire saw more was needed. In November 1965 he named H. Haywood Robbins chairman of a committee to recommend the site, size and cost of a downtown convention and exhibition center. John Belk, who would follow Brookshire as mayor, was a member of the group. Another committee with the same charge was named in April 1968 with lawyer Robert Lassiter as its chairman.

The 1966 Greater Charlotte Central Area Plan, put together by architect A. G. Odell Jr., called for a downtown civic center and trade mart, hotels, with a zoo and sports stadium off West Trade. The report also called for elimination of on-street parking, additional downtown parking, open space at the Square, a pedestrian mall and downtown residential areas. John A. "Jack" Tate Jr., then an NCNB senior vice president, in early 1966 became chairman of the committee to promote the plan.

Tate, who lost to Brookshire in the 1967 mayor's race by only 43 votes, said in 1993 that Odell's plan was "unbelievably sound. It was an outstanding plan. We predicted $100 million of development within 10 years and it occurred in four to five years." Tate was still an uptown advocate in the 1990s and said he was very, very disappointed that the new Charlotte Coliseum wasn't built uptown in the late 1980s. The decision to build it on the outskirts of town "was the biggest government mistake of my lifetime. I'm glad Odell wasn't around to see it." Tate said he also feels more residential development should have been built downtown. One reason he ran against Brookshire was that he didn't think Brookshire was pushing the development of downtown Charlotte as fast as he should.

∞

In January 1966, Brookshire was pushing hard for federal Model Cities funds for the city, using the term "Showcase City." The program was first labeled "demonstration cities" nationally, but President Lyndon Johnson feared that description would tie it to racial demonstrations plaguing the nation's urban areas throughout the mid-1960s. Brookshire asked support from the state's legislative delegation in Washington, but non-committal replies came back very carefully worded, usually saying that Brookshire's and the city's views would be carefully considered. United States Senator Sam Ervin voiced opposition on the grounds that money wasn't available because of the Vietnam War. United States Representative Charles R. Jonas, a conservative Republican, and Brookshire kept the postal service busy with their letters going back and forth on the subject. One of Jonas' replies went on for five single-spaced pages. Jonas was concerned that the program would be superimposed on existing programs and that the deficit was already out of hand. Nevertheless, the exchange of letters remained cordial and Jonas arranged for Brookshire to be part of a panel of mayors who testified for the Model Cities program before a sub-committee of the U.S. House Appropriations Committee.

(Coincidentally, I was working for Jonas in 1965–67 and can vividly remember how meticulous he was in giving carefully worded, well-researched and detailed answers to all questions from his constituents and how fair he tried to be to everyone, regardless of their positions on the conservative-liberal political spectrum.)

Former City Manager Veeder said years later that the city, through contacts, had learned about LBJ's plans for the Model Cities program early on and "we got our name in the pot before there was a pot."

Former Charlotte-Mecklenburg School Board Chairman William E. "Bill" Poe years later said that one of his most vivid memories of Brookshire was his knack for knowing about every aid program coming out of Johnson's administration. "He (Brookshire) was always there with his palm stretched out," Poe said. Poe went on to say that Charlotte was "very fortunate to have them (Brookshire and his successor John Belk) back to back. They were both visionary. Those were exceptional circumstances (having the two available to serve at City Hall)."

The city formally applied for a Model Cities grant in April 1967 and was notified in November 1967 that it was one of 63 cities to receive planning funds. The $172,000 was to plan for improvements in the areas of housing, health, schools, crime prevention and parks in a 1,560-acre area east and west of North Tryon Street. Greenville, First Ward, Belmont and portions of Fourth Ward and Villa Heights were also included.

The city would seek some $50 million in implementation funds for improving the 1,560-acre area on the northern edge of the central core, which had some 26,000 citizens, 20,000 of them black. The city in early 1968 got the $172,000 grant for planning. Some 1,500 people and hundreds and hundreds of pages of paperwork were involved by 1968. The emphasis was to be on housing and relocation, education, social services, job training and employment and physical improvements to parks, streets, etc.

Through the years Charlotte would not be spared the squabbles over who would control the Model Cities programs—Washington, local governments or the citizens themselves. Brookshire drew criticism from radio commentator Jesse Helms' WRAL radio program in mid-1967 over Model Cities. At the same time, Helms praised Congressman Jonas' opposition. Charlotte lawyer Mark Bernstein wrote City Manager Veeder in 1969 that officials in Washington were concerned that officials of the Charlotte Area Fund and Model Cities programs could not agree on their respective roles in the target area. By November, federal HUD and Office of Economic Opportunity officials in Washington told Model Cities and Charlotte Area Fund officials to stop their in-fighting.

Paul Jones, then 39, was plucked out of the U.S. Housing and Urban Development Department in early 1968 to head the local Model Cities program. He came highly touted and was strongly supported by Brookshire and Veeder for the first few months. He seemed to charm Charlotte, yet by May 1968 he charged that the local school system was a "treadmill that assumes slum children are stupid and is organized to keep them off the streets," according to *The Charlotte Observer*. School Board Member Dan Hood said school officials considered the charges "a lie." This started Jones' slide from the highly popular position he had won at the beginning of his time here.

Veeder admitted 25 years later that hiring Jones as director was a mistake—"my mistake." Jones ended up working in the Nixon administration after resigning from his position in Charlotte in mid-1970 after Brookshire had yielded the mayor's chair to his successor, John Belk.

∞

Incidentally, Brookshire turned down an appointment to a top U.S. Housing and Urban Development post in 1967 because he didn't want to move to Washington.

∞

In August of 1966 Brookshire called on private developers to build 400 units of low-cost housing within three to four years. The housing, he said, would go for those displaced by urban renewal, expressways and enforcement of the minimum housing code. In addition, Brookshire said, this would mean the city could cut back its plans for 1,000 public housing units in Charlotte's First Ward and Greenville neighborhoods.

∞

In late 1966, city voters approved $11.4 million in a bond package for urban renewal, airport improvements, a police headquarters building and street improvements, but voted down the $2.5 million to be spent on acquisition of land for a civic center. But, then, in February 1967 a 60-acre governmental center was approved.

∞

Not long before he left office, Brookshire named industrialist Oliver Rowe to head his public housing committee and challenged the group not only to find sites, but oversee equitable distribution, architectural acceptability, open space, school facilities and economic effects.

At the time, the city's public housing inventory consisted of Piedmont Courts, Fairview Homes, Southside Homes, Belvedere Homes, Earle Village, Edwin Towers and two leased housing projects. Proposed were Strawn, Dalton, Barringer Drive, Boulevard, Wilson-Bullard and three leased housing projects.

∞

Brookshire called on Southern Railway officials in Washington to remove the rail lines that stymied downtown development. The president of the railway company was polite but cool to Brookshire's requests and told the mayor that his company was not interested in commercial development. But Brookshire didn't give up. He wrote a letter thanking the president for his time and requested another meeting. This time, some of the railway's vice presidents were present and they were more open to Charlotte's request. A feasibility study was made and Southern Railway came up with a plan not too different from the original Odell plan.

Southern Railway made its proposal in October 1967 for a raised mall and civic center. The following August a private corporation said it would build a $35 million elevated mall and civic center on 25 downtown acres. The city had to widen College, Brevard, Second, Third and other streets as its part of the bargain. Southern Railway removed its warehouses and all but one of its spur lines.

∞

By 1968, the $13.2 million urban renewal program for a key portion of downtown Charlotte had been stalled for two years. The area involved was the 12 blocks east of Trade and Tryon. The federal government finally approved a three-block plan in 1970 and it was here that the Civic Center and NCNB Plaza were eventually constructed. The

Greenville project of nearly 275 acres got $6.1 million for urban renewal in May 1968. The area involved was bounded by Oaklawn Avenue, the Seaboard Airline Railroad, Statesville Avenue and Irwin Creek.

∞

A 1968 plan called for a $35 million merchandise mart to be built on 25 acres south and east of the Square by private investors, the Charlotte Development Association. The plan would consist of apartments, two office towers, a hotel and a motel between Second and Trade, College and Brevard. NCNB was to build a computer center there. By March 1969 the city and the association reached agreement whereby the city and county would build the civic center. Brookshire predicted in mid-1968 that a civic center would be built within three years and would be on a Convention Boulevard. Such was not the case and the boulevard plan was subsequently abandoned.

∞

Brookshire never was to lose his interest in the city and its development. And he was not reluctant to press his positions through letters to the editor in *The Charlotte Observer* and in conversations with the city's business and political leaders.

Just a few months before he died in 1990, Brookshire came to City Hall and asked Ann Marsh to type a letter for him and make sure it was distributed to City Council members. "I guess I knew it might be the last time I would see him for he told me he had not been feeling well. Anyway, I kept a copy of this letter," she said.

The letter said, in part:

"The recommendation made last week by the Urban Land Institute Group to expand our Convention Center at its present location, rather than abandoning it (at an economic loss) and build a new one seems to make a lot of sense.

"The present location is in the heart of the city, only a block from four major hotels (Marriott, Radisson, Days Inn and the new, nearly completed Omni)—an important consideration from the viewpoint of convention and trade show visitors. The proposed new location at College and Stonewall would be three to four blocks from these hotels and not close to any existing or proposed hotels . . .

"It appears to me that by bridging the railroad, the block down to Brevard (largely vacant) would be ample land on which to build the addition. The steep decline in the contour of that block would lend itself to a design of three to four floors, or perhaps more if necessary.

"The Convention Center at its present location was the keystone of our 1966 Master Plan for the core city and deserves to keep its premier location. Moving it to a more remote location would diminish Charlotte's new face."

Brookshire's advice was not heeded, of course. He died less than four months later.

∞

By the time Brookshire left office in 1969, 18 miles of overhead lines had been removed. The $15 million, 32-story First Union tower was under construction, 6,881 substandard dwellings had been demolished and 13,950 dwellings had been brought up to minimum code—but 10,000 substandard dwelling units still existed. The city had acquired $100 million in federal funds for the downtown area. Second, Third, Fourth, Trade, College, Brevard and McDowell streets had been widened. With the help of Councilman Bryant, Assistant City Manager Carstarphen, and others, downtown beautification, including tree plantings, had occurred. And 263 acres of slums were gone.

∞

Long after he left office and only a few years before he died, Brookshire wrote *The Charlotte Observer* to propose a park—"an oasis of green"—with lots of greenery in front and shops along the rear at the southwest corner of Trade and Tryon. He appeared on the Charlotte Issues Forum on cable television to explain and discuss his proposal. On that forum, he lamented that the suburban malls had doomed Charlotte's uptown retail trade.

Chapter Five

Roads—Where They Were Built and Why

Certainly the most drama involving transportation issues of the Brookshire years centered on the so-called belt road.

The inner belt, proposed in November 1957, was the subject of countless meetings, negotiations and dramatic votes. This road, designated as Charlotte 4, would eventually stretch from North Tryon Street in the northeast to Interstate 85 on the westside, along Eastway, Wendover and Woodlawn roads and the Billy Graham Parkway.

Actually, a belt road and a civic center really were first recommended to the Chamber of Commerce by City Planner John Nolen back in 1917, but were never acted upon. Nolen also proposed parkways down Sugar, Irwin and Stewart creeks. The 1960 Master Thoroughfare Plan called for a full expressway loop around the downtown area.

Councilman Steve Dellinger took sharp exception to Mayor Brookshire's call in March 1964 for an update of the belt road plans and said the delay was unnecessary. "It's time we started expediting rather than experting," Dellinger said. Brookshire also took heat from several councilmen after he asked for advice from Wilbur Smith and Associates without informing the council first.

Councilman Claude Albea, who lived on North Tryon Street, was the only member of council not affected in some way or other by the belt road routes that had been suggested, although Councilman John Thrower said the impact on his house off Woodlawn was minimal.

Councilman Gibson Smith, who later ran for mayor against Brookshire and John Belk, charged in March 1964 that State Highway Commissioner Paul Younts said he "would blast me with both barrels if I don't shut up about the belt road." Smith said Younts had been a good public servant, but "he wants that road through or he'll bust." Smith argued that a Wendover route would doom the Myers Park residential area. The Charlotte-Mecklenburg Board of Education also got into the act, saying a route suggested by Myers Park residents attempting to steer the belt road route away from their homes would endanger students at Oakhurst Elementary and Smith Junior High. Smith argued that the outer belt ought to be tackled even before the route of the inner belt was determined. He said the outer belt might make the inner belt unnecessary.

School officials also opposed the portion of the route through the Myers Park-Alexander Graham school complex. Saxby Chaplin, president of the student body at Myers Park High School in 1964 and an attorney in Charlotte in 1994, said the issue was a hot topic at his school. "It doesn't have them standing on the tables or anything. But there's a lot of talk against the road," he told *The Charlotte News* in 1964. Most of the concern centered on what the road might do to the Myers Park athletic fields.

The issue was definitely emotional. Mrs. Elisha Carter of 1464 Wendover said she had lived on the street as long as anyone and said the belt would jeopardize lives. "Do you know what it is to hold a dying child in your arms? Well, I do. The last word I heard was, 'Momma.'" Another opponent said Wendover would end up with worse traffic than Independence Boulevard. State highway officials argued— in vain at the time but prophetically—that the street would more nearly resemble Selwyn Avenue.

Clarence E. Beeson, president of the Myers Park Country Club, said the directors were adamantly against a suggestion in April that the belt road go across the club's golf course. Builder Charles Ervin had offered to buy 75 acres of the Myers Park Club. Ervin's plan was to build housing on 75 acres of the site, let the belt go through the development—with the club building a new golf course farther out, yet retaining a nine-hole course and its clubhouse at the old site. Ervin said he made his proposal in response to a request from Brookshire and City Manager Veeder.

Council on May 4 voted 5-1, with Bryant casting the negative vote and Dellinger absent, to put the belt down Briar Creek and across the golf course, rather than by the schools and along Wendover. State highway officials had estimated the golf course route at $2 million and the school route at $4 million. Attorney (and later Federal Judge) James McMillan and J. Ed Burnside, former president of the Charlotte Chamber of Commerce and a good friend of Brookshire, were among those against the council decision.

Brookshire revealed the next day—May 5—that Ervin had formally offered $1 million for 73 acres of the club. Ervin had made his offer at a secret council gathering at Sandy Jordan's home on the Sunday afternoon two days before. It was on the basis of Ervin's offer that the council made its decision the day before, Brookshire said. Ervin said the $1 million would allow the club to build another 18-acre course, while retaining a nine-hole course and the club house on the existing site. Ervin contended that both the club and the school-Wendover routes would cost the same, about $2.4 million. Beeson again announced the club's opposition and threatened a court battle if the city persisted.

Ervin withdrew his offer May 22 in the face of the Myers Park Club's unwavering stand. Then, Myers Park Club officials said a move would cost $2.5 million, two-and-a-half times Ervin's estimate. Beeson, in a letter to club members, said this would mean club dues would go up 46 percent. Beeson kept the issue hot by saying in July that the club membership was "overwhelmingly" against the belt route that the council had selected back in May. City council didn't alter that decision despite the withdrawal of Ervin's offer.

Meanwhile, sources told *The Charlotte News* in August that a State Highway Department study, then in the works, would say that Wendover was the only practical route because of cost. That meant that the Whittington-Thrower-Albea-Dellinger majority would eventually switch the route to Wendover. Early in September, it was learned that Younts was working on a compromise that would mean the belt would be approved—but with a gap of 1.7 miles or 2.2 miles in the middle. How the gap would be filled was to be determined within five to seven years. Jim McDuffie, who later was to serve on City Council and in the General Assembly and who lived on Eastway Drive, strongly objected. It was learned in late September that Younts gave the council an ultimatum—make a decision on the belt or lose $10 million in state money earmarked for it. Younts on

September 21 formally gave the council three choices—a Wendover, Sharon Road and Runneymede Lane route; approving the belt with a gap to be filled by 1970; or, abandon the idea. By then, insiders were saying it looked as if three and maybe four (Dellinger being the question mark) favored the Wendover route. "Don't stake yourself out on anything," one councilman told a reporter. "Anything can happen this week."

On September 28, council voted 4-3 for the gap proposal. Bryant, Dellinger, Jordan and Smith were in the majority. The gap was determined to be two miles long and was to be filled by 1970. Wendover residents cheered as Jordan hesitantly put up the fourth hand, but Albea warned the decision would come back to haunt the council. Thrower predicted the road would never be built.

Just before the September vote, council received a petition from then Garinger High School teacher Laura Frech (later a City Council member) urging approval of a belt road. John Belk, who was to follow Brookshire as mayor but was then president of the Chamber of Commerce, also wrote council members to urge approval of the belt road. Belk was representing the chamber.

Just after the vote, McDuffie circulated a petition to recall Smith, Bryant, Jordan and Dellinger. McDuffie also collected nearly 1,500 write-in votes for his alias "Phil Gap" for a number of offices in the general election in November 1964.

Beeson said in November that the council was misleading the public and predicted the belt would eventually go across the golf course.

The final 4-3 vote selecting Wendover Road—instead of the golf course path or a gap—for the middle link came November 30, 1964, with Whittington, Albea, Thrower and Jordan in the majority and Bryant, Dellinger and Smith voting against the proposal. The 4-3 vote resulted when Jordan surprised all his colleagues in reversing himself from his support of the Briar Creek route September 28. Jordan had informed the other council members in a darkened council chamber shortly before the council meeting started. Wendover Road residents, including Duke Power Company's Carl Horn Jr., were outraged. They said that in addition to the undesirable increase in traffic, a widened Wendover would destroy the oaks lining the street. Younts and Pete McKnight, editor of *The Charlotte Observer*, were said to have been the leaders in pressuring Jordan to switch his vote.

Years later, Bryant said the whole issue was "a fascinating exercise because of all the factors involved." Thrower said more pressure was brought to bear on him on that issue than any other. Whittington also listed it as one of the big issues of his many years at City Hall, but noted that Wendover still has its oaks.

This was not the end, however. With the help of a lawsuit, the position of Highway Commissioner George Broadrick and Jim "Phil Gap" McDuffie, construction along Wendover was delayed until 1976.

∞

About the same time, September 28, 1964, the council unanimously voted to start on an outer belt in the Tyvola Road, Carmel Road and Rama Road area, connecting with Beam Road on the west and I-85 on the east. The prediction was the belt would avoid the controversy that had surrounded the inner belt for so long.

∞

Former City Traffic Engineer Herman Hoose said years later that the mayors and city councils routinely updated the master plan year after year until the administration of Ken Harris, who succeeded Belk. Hoose blamed former City Councilman—and subsequently Mayor—Harvey Gantt, "He didn't believe in roads."

Sue Myrick, who was Charlotte's mayor in 1987–91 and who had a major interest in roads, credited Brookshire for seeing the need for belt roads before anyone else. "Others thought it was crazy to talk about a loop around the city," she said.

∞

Less controversial, but significant was Brookshire's call in January for improvements to Third, Fourth, Fifth, Sixth, 28th, Brevard and Caldwell streets.

∞

Hoose, who was the city's traffic engineer for 30 years and during all of Brookshire's and Belk's time in City Hall, said City Manager Veeder was "a highway man!" The feisty former city official, still advising other cities on traffic matters in 1993 at the age of 82, said Brookshire and his successor were transportation oriented—his kind of mayors.

Hoose fought through the years for parking bans in the downtown area. He got the angle parking taken off portions of Trade and Tryon in the 1950s and in early 1963 was seeking more restrictions. The Chamber of Commerce backed Hoose and this was evidenced through a letter on behalf of the chamber from John Belk, who was the first vice president. And Earl Crawford Jr., then executive vice president of the Downtown Charlotte Association, argued that the streets were there to move traffic, not store cars. But small merchants in the downtown area opposed the restrictions. City Council postponed the decision week after week and drew criticism from *The Charlotte Observer* for its collective procrastination. Finally, in September 1963 the council voted more restrictions on a trial basis, but not extending the peak-hour ban.

Hoose also established Charlotte's first traffic islands, thereby earning the nickname "Thousand Islands Hoose."

∞

Just before Brookshire took office, the corner of Graham and Trade was cited as "the meanest intersection" in the city. The heavy flow of traffic had resulted in 39 accidents the previous year as 27,000 vehicles (including 5,400 trucks) passed through and 4,000 pedestrians crossed the intersection between 7 a.m. and 7 p.m.

∞

Hoose pushed for a walkway over Fourth Street between the County Courthouse and the new County Office Building, but he opposed the suggestion of merchant George Dowdy of Belk to have a mid-block crosswalk across College from the downtown Belk store to a parking lot.

∞

Then, in December 1961 Hoose closed 22 streets that intersected with Independence Boulevard to through traffic and left turns.

∞

Brookshire on several occasions opposed council's decisions to rezone portions of Independence Boulevard from residential and office uses to business use—against the advice of the planners. He warned that too much traffic would be generated and the boulevard would be doomed. Years later, Whittington likewise said he had fought to keep Independence from Pecan to Morningside zoned for office and institutional, not commercial uses, but failed—to the detriment of the strip.

∞

Brookshire was able to report in 1966 that the city completed the Sugar Creek, Eastway, Woodlawn and Sharon Amity road projects.

∞

In September 1964, the city condemned 1629 Elizabeth, owned by Brookshire, for what would eventually be the Belk Freeway.

∞

(To show how much the city has changed, Brookshire recalled years later that he was able to ride his horse on an unpaved Randolph Road to the Mint Museum as late as the 1950s. Though several others interviewed for this book doubted this, realtor T.R. Lawing confirmed it and said he also remembered when Colville Road was unpaved.)

Chapter Six

What Charlotte Had Was Really a Small-Town Airport

In the Brookshire years, the Charlotte airport terminal and parking lot out front were very small compared with the terminal and parking facilities of 1994. It was not uncommon to be able to park so close you would only have to walk 50 to 100 yards from your car to the terminal building. The uncovered lot was smaller than the Cotswold Mall parking lot of 1994. In fact, it is not much of an exaggeration to say that the lobby was so small you could see everyone in it from any one place. The Dogwood Room restaurant was on the second floor.

The terminal building and parking lot were still there in 1994, near the end of West Boulevard, and served a variety of uses. The $2-million, 74,000-square-foot terminal had opened in 1954 and the airport at that time was named Douglas Municipal Airport. The "Douglas" stood for the late Charlotte Mayor Ben E. Douglas Sr., who served as mayor from 1936 to 1941 and is often referred to as the father of aviation in Charlotte. When Douglas came to

Charlotte in 1925, the city enjoyed daily airmail service, but most airplanes used a privately owned dirt runway off Tuckaseegee Road or one of the other smaller private airports. The airport was privately owned and used on weekends for air shows and war pilot training until the city took it over in 1935. Eastern provided the first regularly scheduled passenger service, beginning in 1937. The Army Air Force took control of the airport in 1941 and established Morris Field Air Base.

It was renamed Charlotte/Douglas International Airport when the new terminal opened in 1982. By 1992, the size of the terminal totaled one million square feet.

∞

Boardings totaled 363,191 in 1960 and jumped to 377,472 in 1961. At that time it was predicted that boardings would reach 480,000 by 1970. The actual number in 1970 was 814,614! Airport boardings were 737,741 in 1968, Brookshire's last full year in office. A strike of airline machinists in 1966 had resulted in boardings falling from 576,320 to 561,665 that year—to the dismay of local boosters.

∞

The city was pushing hard for jet service in early 1961 as J. Ed Burnside, chairman of the Chamber of Commerce's aviation committee, and Mayor James Smith (this was just before the election in which Brookshire won the office) led a local delegation to call on Delta Airlines to seek such service. The thrust of their argument to Delta and other airlines was that the first airline to provide jet service here would have a major competitive edge in Charlotte.

∞

At about the time of the 1961 election an outside consultant recommended that a jet runway be added and the terminal be expanded. A year later, the city did move on a $2.5 million improvement plan, which included extending the north-south runway, but not terminal expansion.

∞

In June 1961 the city landed a plum—the $6 million Eastern Airlines Reservation Center to be located on the old Black Dairy Farm at the corner of Fairview and Park roads. Eastern Airline officials said Charlotte was selected, in part, because of its excellent record in the race relations field. Former veteran City Councilman Jim Whittington in 1993 credited Eastern Airlines with having a major, lasting and positive effect on Charlotte through the airport and said its demise was a "tragedy" for Charlotte and the Southeast.

∞

The city was excited in late 1961 when five jetliners landed at the local airport after bad weather diverted them from Atlanta.

The city got its first scheduled jet service in 1962, provided by Eastern Airlines. Local publications claimed that "theater enthusiasts could attend a play in New York City and be back by midnight—almost."

∞

Manager Al Quinn resigned as airport manager in early 1962 after six controversial years at the post. He cited low pay as his reason, but pressure had been building against him.

Years later, former City Manager Bill Veeder recalled his surprise at being informed that the Charlotte Aero Club was honoring him as "Airport Man of the Year" for 1962. Veeder noted that he "hadn't done anything to deserve the honor." He was told that he had been selected because he got rid of the airport manager the group was not pleased with.

Tom Rafferty was hired away from Long Beach, California, in May 1962 at a salary of $13,380 and served with distinction for five years before leaving for San Antonio. He and Veeder worked closely and well together through those years.

∞

Eastern Airlines' strike in the summer of 1962 cut into revenues, but the airport income still went up over the previous year.

∞

Included in a $12.6 million bond referendum approved by the voters in September 1962 was $1.5 million for the airport. Brookshire reported at year's end in 1963 that the contract for the second runway at the airport had been let. Two concourses were added in Brookshire's tenure at City Hall. A $2 million expansion project at the airport was completed in 1964. Some $600,000 more in improvements were coming. A new air freight terminal was built in 1966.

∞

Charles L. Sweitzer got permission to paint a mural tracing the history of the area within the terminal during 1963. He used models from North Carolina, including Governor Terry Sanford and evangelist Billy Graham among many, many others. But the mural later ran into bitter controversy because it contained scenes that many thought were demeaning to blacks. When asked about it later, then Airport Manager R.C. "Josh" Birmingham said the mural "died a natural death."

∞

Ross Knight was named to replace Rafferty in early 1967 and he served until he died in 1970. Edwin Petro served for less than a year before handing over the post to Birmingham, who held the top airport post through the remainder of the Belk years and until 1988.

∞

Brookshire cut the ribbon in March 1967 for a $500,000 west concourse. Rafferty had left for San Antonio earlier in 1967 but came back for the ceremony.

∞

In November 1968, Brookshire suggested the county take over the airport because it had a higher debt limit. Nothing came of the suggestion.

∞

The Federal Aviation Administration allocated $215,000 in fiscal year 1969 for a taxiway.

Chapter Seven

Planning, Reports, and Related Items—What Worked and What Didn't

Mayor Brookshire in January 1962 urged council to put restrictions on floodplain use. Councilman Don Bryant then suggested in mid-1962 that the city buy undeveloped floodplain land for park use. One site suggested was between Providence and Sharon roads, Hanson Drive and Briar Creek. Luxurious houses and a day care center occupied the land in 1994. And the general area still experienced some flooding when Charlotte got hit by heavy rains, but not nearly as serious as in the 1960s and 1970s. The U.S. Army Corps of Engineers conducted a study of local problems along Sugar and Briar creeks in 1964.

∞

In September 1964, City-County Planning Director William McIntyre took me, then a *Charlotte News* reporter, on a tour of the city's floodplains, which he saw as a potential seven-mile greenway or "necklace" round the city. One spot where we stopped was a wooded area out on

Monroe Road, which McIntyre said would be wonderful for a park as large as Freedom Park. He suggested a driving range, tennis courts and a lake but not soccer fields and jogging trails! These were sports with virtually zero popularity in Charlotte in 1964 but that later became the predominant attractions at McAlpine Greenway Park.

∞

The City Council rezoned the city's entire 120 square miles under a new zoning ordinance in Brookshire's first term. Council members met twice a week for two months as they looked at every tract in the city.

∞

City Council in April 1964 got a consultant's report calling for a city-county law enforcement center and a courthouse devoted entirely to judicial activities. No cost estimates were provided, but the projects were to be completed by 1966. The following month, another consultant's report called for broader powers for the city manager, including the authority to name the fire chief and police chief. At that time, the City Council named the police and fire chiefs and the city attorney while the city manager named the other department heads.

∞

Dr. Reginald Hawkins, a black activist who ran for governor in 1968 and 1972, sought throughout the early 1960s to open Good Samaritan Hospital, which was at 801 South Graham Street, to all races, and to have black doctors and dentists be able to practice at all other Charlotte-Mecklenburg hospitals.

(Ironically, Dr. Martin Luther King Jr. was to have been campaigning for Hawkins' gubernatorial race in North Carolina April 4, 1968, but postponed his trip to the state, saying he needed to remain in Memphis because of the situation regarding the garbage strike there. It was there that King was assassinated by James Earl Ray.)

The Ladies Church Aid Society of St. Peter's Episcopal Church had originally established the hospital in 1888. It was said to be the first hospital in the world for Negroes. By the 1950s, it was an anachronism because of being ill-equipped and understaffed. The city had taken the hospital over from the North Carolina Episcopal Diocese for $1 in July 1961. (Signs of the times—*The Charlotte News*, in a story about the action, wrote that " . . . 30 percent of Charlotte's population which is *colored* . . . ") Years later, City Manager Veeder called conditions at Good Samaritan "a mess" when the city took it over. "The church may have done a good thing initially, but they turned over a disaster to the city," he said.

An $800,000 renovation project for Good Samaritan Hospital approved in a bond vote was held up in 1960 because Negro citizens feared such work would only per-petuate the facility's segregated status. Brookshire issued a statement promising to push for opening the hospitals to all citizens, but called on Negroes to be patient. After much debate over funding and how the money should be spent, the price tag on the renovation totaled $1.3 million two years later. The shortfall was made up by surplus city funds and a grant from the Duke Endowment.

In March 1962, Hawkins led picketing of Charlotte Memorial, Good Samaritan, Mercy and Presbyterian hospi-tals. After weeks of demonstrations Good Samaritan (re-named Charlotte Community Hospital in November 1963) admitted its first white patient on an emergency basis (other white patients had been treated there, but not admitted). The news media and white politicians at the time reported that there was little evidence that Hawkins had broad support. Brookshire responded to Hawkins by saying he was not sympathetic and that "belligerent acts of pressure will result in building resentments and antagonisms."

Hawkins continued his battle through letters to Attorney General Robert F. Kennedy and through the courts, finally calling for a strike of doctors at Good Samaritan in the spring of 1963. The Public Health Service, which made three investigations, did find Memorial guilty of discrimination in admissions, even though it had undertaken token integration in 1960. Under the threat of having a $4.2-million construction program halted by the federal government, Memorial was opened to patients and doctors of all races. Mercy and particularly Presbyterian lagged behind in opening up their facilities. Charlotte Memorial's move to a desegregated status in September 1963 caused Good Samaritan to lose patients.

A 1964 report, this one by the Charlotte-Mecklenburg Hospital Authority and the Duke Endowment, went to council the same month and recommended that the then all-Negro Charlotte Community Hospital accept all patients as a matter of policy. Council reaction was cool to the idea, which carried a $90,000 price tag.

Council members later were critical of the hospital authority after the authority washed its hands of Community Hospital. Councilman Steve Dellinger accused the authority of "leading us along like a blind mule to the end of the road and left us no where to turn around."

In early November 1964, council voted to convert the hospital to serve long-term, chronic-disease patients and to be placed under the hospital authority. The details of the transfer were not completed until April 1966.

Edward R. Frye's resignation as hospital administrator was greeted with relief throughout much of the black community when it came in 1965.

The hospital was closed in May 1981, but was used later, before being torn down, as a rest home under the name of The Magnolias.

∞

The population of the city was 201,564 in 1960. In June 1964, the City-County Planning Commission predicted Charlotte would have 315,000 residents by 1970. The population at the time was 224,428. The actual total in 1970 turned out to be 241,178.

In January 1965, it was predicted that the city would have 250,000 in 1968—the actual total turned out to be 234,140.

The largest annexation during the Brookshire period was in 1965 when 9,042 people and 4.5 square miles between South Boulevard and Sharon Road were brought into the city.

∞

A $21.1 million bond package—the largest to date—was approved by the voters in January 1965. It was aimed at needs caused by what Brookshire called "the explosive growth" in the previous few years and specifically was used to make progress on the expressway system, water and sewer facilities, a police headquarters and urban renewal.

∞

It was also at this time that Brookshire proudly announced that City Hall got its first computer!

∞

Brookshire named a nine-member Charter Review Commission in August 1963. Attorney Joseph W. Grier Jr. later was named chairman. The task before it was to rewrite the 1939 charter, which City Attorney John Morrisey said had been patched so many times it had patches on the patches.

The commission voted in February to take away the mayor's power to break ties on council votes, then reversed itself in October and restored the mayor's vote. The Charter Review Commission's report issued in early August of 1964 called for abolishment of the Park and Recreation Commission and for the Auditorium-Coliseum Authority to be replaced by an advisory board under the control and operation of City Council. The commission also recommended that all department heads be appointed by the city manager—not just some of them. Brookshire agreed with these recommendations, but City Council, except for Don Bryant, did not. The charter approved by City Council in March 1965 left the division of powers about where it had been. After several weeks of haggling between the city and the local legislative delegation, the charter bill was introduced in Raleigh and finally approved by the General Assembly in late May 1965.

∞

Brookshire and County Commission Chairman Jim Martin were instrumental in setting up the Regional Council of Governments (called the Centralina Council of Governments in 1994) in late 1967 and early 1968. The U.S. Department of Housing and Urban Development had urged the establishment of the voluntary group to identify problems and opportunities and provide a forum for discussion of both.

∞

The term "Metrolina" was unveiled for the 12-county market area in 1968.

Chapter Eight

A Grab Bag—Bond Issues and Blue Laws

Mayor Stan Brookshire had barely taken office when three leaders of the Charlotte Women's Club—Doris Cromartie, Mrs. L.E. Barnhardt and Mrs. Edward T. Klerlein—called on him to urge that more women be named to city boards.

∞

In early 1964 the State Supreme Court upheld the city's Sunday sales law, which banned sale of consumer items on Sundays. Local discount houses remained open as the decision was being processed, but Clark's and Atlantic Mills started closing in late February because of the law, which had actually been passed in September 1962. Implementation had been held up in the courts between 1962 and 1964. Strangely enough to merchants and shoppers alike in 1994, the vast majority of merchants in those days really didn't want to open on Sundays. Religion, custom and lack of greed all played a part in their position. Nevertheless the merchants didn't provide strong public support to council members who were trying to maintain the sales law.

Councilman Don Bryant brought the issue up again March 9 and said that "a law is a law only if the people accept it." When he announced his switch just before the council met, Bryant said he made the decision "because apparently I have misjudged the desires of the citizens of Charlotte." He said the overwhelming number of calls he received were in opposition to the law.

The sales law was repealed by a 4-3 vote when Bryant and Sandy Jordan switched their votes and joined Jim Whittington and John Thrower for a majority. Thrower said the sales law was hypocritical and he believed the city had no business legislating morality. *The Charlotte News* had gone to press before the vote was taken, but with a large front-page headline saying, "Council To Repeal Sunday Sales Ban." The second paragraph said that a majority went into "this afternoon's meeting prepared to vote for repeal of the sales ban." To the relief of reporters and editors, that's what happened. The law had been enforced three Sundays resulting in six arrests. City Council had allowed the sale of certain so-called necessary items such as toilet paper on Sundays. The shoppers flocked back to the stores when they reopened—very clearly showing their feelings on the issue with their shopping habits.

City Hall observers said at the time that the Sunday sales law and the belt road controversy created more havoc around City Hall than any other issues in history. Bryant, Jordan and Thrower all reported middle-of-the-night calls on the Sunday sales issue. Bryant said one night he got 25 calls between midnight and 7 a.m. The councilmen said some of the callers were "abusive and lewd."

∞

In a somewhat related occurrence, Hobart Smith Construction Co. had announced in 1963 that it would no longer show houses on Sundays, but would beef up its sales efforts on other days. The company was sticking to its policy 30 years later, but it was a rarity.

∞

The City Council held a public hearing November 10, 1964, on the question of allowing cable television, then referred to as community antenna television (CATV), to move into the city. Cable television had begun about 10 years before as a "mom and pop" business in small communities, mostly in the western part of the nation. The first clipping on the subject in the files at *The Charlotte Observer* had a lead that read, "Community antenna television—a dream or a sugar-coated nightmare?" The story warned that CATV could prevent cities from getting additional stations, could kill radio, and could put merchants out of business. The story did not elaborate on the latter threat. The story predicted installation at $10–$20 with rental at $5–$9 a month. WSOC-TV and WBTV both warned at the time that the city's drive to get a third channel might be jeopardized if cable television were allowed. Critics wondered why anyone would want to pay for television when all three networks soon would be available. Yes, that's what they said and few laughed!

(Yet in March 1993, Tele-Communications Incorporated, the nation's largest cable television company, announced new technology would allow it to deliver 500 channels in 1994. Again, it was asked—do viewers really want all those choices?)

Then, in April 1966 Jefferson Standard Broadcasting (WBTV) said it wanted to build a CATV system in Charlotte. Two months later, WSOC-TV said it also wanted to build a system in Charlotte. In July 1966 WCCB-TV moved to Channel 18. WCTU, the station that would eventually become WCNC-TV, went on the air a year later. WCCB-TV subsequently lent its backing to the idea of having cable television here, but Channel 36 and theater owners opposed it.

In November 1966, City Council finally agreed with the proposition of having cable television in Charlotte, while some were saying the license agreement could be established so that a financial bonanza to the city would result.

WBTV, WSOC-TV, WCTU and Television Transmission Company of New York all expressed an interest in March 1967 with WBTV and WSOC-TV both being awarded contracts. They were urged to merge, but instead the two battled before the Federal Communications Commission. Finally, on September 27, 1967, Cablevision of Charlotte, owned by Jefferson Carolina Corporation (WBTV), made its first cable television sale in Charlotte. The installation fee was $10 and the monthly fee was $4.95. The WSOC-TV entry was operating a month later in another geographic area of the city. The two cable outfits decided between themselves how to divide the city.

Brookshire was deeply involved in the issue and was instrumental in getting council members with various views on the matter to come to a consensus that he believed would be in the best interests of city government and the citizens.

Former City Attorney John Morrisey recalled in 1993 that the law was fuzzy at the time on what authority city government had in regulating cable television. James W. Kiser, who succeeded Morrisey and who inherited the problem from him, agreed that a great deal of research had to be done to make sure the city did not get itself in the same situation as other cities had—with court cases filed by those whose applications were rejected. Kiser said in 1993 that the ordinance avoided litigation by saying that anyone could apply and one or more franchises would be granted. If one applicant did not get a license, the application could be re-drafted and submitted again.

∞

Central Piedmont Community College was born in 1963 in a merger of Mecklenburg College and the Industrial Education Center. Charlotte College became the fourth campus of the University of North Carolina system in 1965.

∞

Brookshire voiced concern over newspaper liquor ads—to no avail—in 1965.

∞

Brookshire named a committee to deal with the problems of obscenity, but the committee, headed by lawyer Paul Ervin, reported in mid-1965 that voluntary action, not censorship, was the answer to the problem.

∞

Calls for consolidation echoed throughout City Hall and the County Courthouse through the Brookshire years . . . and Belk years . . . and beyond . . .

Years later, former County Commission Chairman Charles M. Lowe said Brookshire believed that the county taxpayers didn't pay their fair share "and he was not wrong!" Lowe said county commissioners then and into the 1990s seemed to think they are elected to represent only those residents outside the city limits, even though a majority of the county residents, as well as the county commissioners, live within the city and most of the wealth is there. Lowe said he and Brookshire constantly tried to bring the other commissioners around to their thinking.

Brookshire proved himself a reliable prophet when he warned in 1966 that total consolidation was a long way off, but a consolidation committee was appointed in 1968–69. The mayor addressed the issue of consolidation of parks, police and water in a major speech in March 1967.

In 1968, Morrisey, by then executive director of the North Carolina Association of County Commissioners, told Jay Jenkins of *The Charlotte Observer* that state law precluded resolution of many problems confronting local governments.

"You seldom see any change in government in the absence of a crisis and the process of evolution is too slow. We have a crisis today," Jenkins quoted Morrisey as saying.

The crisis, Morrisey said, stemmed from the lack of statutory or constitutional authority for cities and counties to perform tasks thrust upon them. The 100-year-old state constitution limited what the General Assembly could allow local governments to do. For example, local governments couldn't become the community action agency in the war against poverty being pushed by President Lyndon Johnson. State law also inhibited merger of and cooperation between city and county governments, Morrisey said.

∞

Much was made of the mayor's two-week trip to sister city Arequipa, Peru, in February 1962. The sister city program, which had been established by President Dwight D. Eisenhower in 1961, was of great importance to Brookshire, who devoted six pages in his family history to the program and only eight more to all the other matters and issues he faced during his eight years in office.

In the history, Brookshire reported that when he took office, he found an unanswered letter from the mayor of Arequipa suggesting establishment of a sister city relationship. Brookshire later got an official invitation to visit Arequipa. The Peruvian government, with help from Peruvian businesses, offered an expense-paid trip for Brookshire and asked that he bring 25 to 30 others from Charlotte at about $425 each for 10 days. Brookshire put together a party of 25 of his friends to make the trip. While there, he had a surprise breakfast with Charlotte's Billy Graham, who coincidentally was conducting an evangelistic crusade in Lima. Brookshire was asked to sit on the crusade platform that evening and to make a few remarks. Afterward, Brookshire said he presented Graham with a key to the city of Charlotte, quipping that "I had followed him 5,000 miles to make the presentation."

The relationship between Charlotte and Arequipa continued through the years with delegations from Arequipa visiting here in 1964, 1965, 1970 and 1971. Charlotte sent orchestra music "outgrown" by the Charlotte Symphony to Arequipa and even sent Dr. Richard Cormier, the symphony director, there for six weeks in mid-1966 to establish and train a municipal orchestra. Money and 200 surplus school desks were also sent, as well as 10 television sets from the Dilworth Rotary Club. After the desks arrived, the Arequipa mayor requested that Brookshire fly down to receive the city's official thanks. Brookshire tried to beg off, but eventually gave in. Brookshire said when he went over to shake the hands of several hundred cheering poor children he had "an emotional experience in which I could not restrain my tears."

A humorous incident also occurred during the visit and Brookshire reported it in his family history. While visiting in a private home, the mayor was approached by a wealthy divorced Peruvian, who said he was in love with a woman from Lenoir, North Carolina. The man wanted Brookshire to hand-deliver a letter to her. Brookshire reported that "the man said he was sure the North Carolina woman was in love with him 'because she and her husband do not walk together.' I told him I could not do it because I knew the young lady's family, which I do, and that as mayor I could not afford to get involved in an international intrigue! He even wanted Edith (Brookshire's wife) and me to invite the young lady, without her husband, to spend a weekend with us, and he would fly to Charlotte to be with her! The next morning, he was at the airport to see us off to Lima, with gifts of china teapots, bags of tea, and flowers for the ladies. I guess he was not too upset with my unwillingness to cooperate with his little love scheme."

About the time Brookshire left office, Arequipa built a new park and named it Charlotte Park. Brookshire's successor, John Belk, went to Charlotte's sister city for five days in November 1970 for the dedication. As a follow-up, a mini-park was created next to the downtown library and named Arequipa Park. The mayor of Arequipa came to Charlotte for the dedication in November 1971. Coincidentally, Brookshire was president of the Carolinas Carrousel that year and Arequipa was recognized during the annual Thanksgiving Day parade.

Mayor Sue Myrick, who was Charlotte's mayor in 1987–91, credited Brookshire with being very forward thinking in starting the Sister Cities program before the need to Charlotte was obvious. "Now, we have no choice," she said years later. "Then there was no need. But he did it anyway."

∞

In mid-1964 Brookshire led a delegation of Charlotteans to France for that nation's "Salute to Dixie."

∞

Morrisey recalled another interesting incident from the early 1960s. Fred Alexander, not then an elected official, called Morrisey to complain about a West Trade Street homeowner who had a cement wall in front of his house with pieces of glass sticking out of it. Alexander said that the area was inhabited by derelicts and one could easily fall on the wall and cut himself seriously.

Morrisey said he went to see for himself and was horrified and feared for children who might be playing in the area. "I told the owner that I was going to the police station and report it. I said he would be wise to remedy it. I was talking out of my Irish head. I had no statutes or ordinances to cite. But I thought it was a helluva way to protect one's property. He took care of it," Morrisey said.

∞

Shades of the Cold War—Brookshire endorsed the city's civil defense plan, but noted evacuation ought to be voluntary and reminded his fellow citizens that Charlotte was not classified as a prime target and, in fact, was named "a third-rate target."

∞

Brookshire was very interested in beautifying the city and pushed to have trees planted downtown and to plant flowers in medians and at triangles. One of the first projects undertaken, recalled former Assistant City Manager Bill Carstarphen, was the triangle in front of Covenant Presbyterian Church. Carstarphen said that was one of his first assignments—and successes—after joining the City Hall staff in mid-1964. Once again, federal funds were sought and obtained for the project.

∞

At the start of 1965, Brookshire asked Councilman Milton Short to be the point man on extending water lines into the county. At the same time, he asked Alexander to lead the campaign for a public accommodations ordinance and Jerry Tuttle to help revive the downtown area. Short said almost 30 years later that while some suggested generic guidelines were needed, he thought the best approach was to tackle each water extension issue separately. That was what happened as lines were extended to Carowinds, UNC Charlotte, the airport and out Independence Boulevard.

Brookshire, in August 1966, met with County Commission Chairman Sam T. Atkinson and emerged from an 80-minute closed-door meeting to say that they had worked out a joint agreement on water-sewer matters that would end 30 years of wrangling. Atkinson dropped his call for the county to take over the city system and the two agreed that the county would finance new lines, the city would supply the water and treatment facilities and the city would handle the water metering and maintenance. Their colleagues on the council and commission balked, however, and the issue remained unsettled when Brookshire left office in 1969.

Brookshire issued a news release on the last day of 1968 to the effect that while he believed he had been consistent in promoting city-county cooperation in the extension of water-sewer facilities into the developing areas of the county, his position had sometimes been misunderstood. Because of legal issues, he said he opposed all proposals to have the county take over the city's water-sewer system. Brookshire charged that "continuing insistence on the part of the county that it either take over the city's water and sewer system or build one of its own or dictate the terms of a cooperative agreement has resulted in unnecessary delays in meeting the needs in the county, which is unfortunate."

This came after the county had supplied the Westinghouse Corporation with water.

Short said the county grew tired of being in the water and sewer business and the Charlotte-Mecklenburg Utility Department was established in January 1972 with the City Council and County Commission jointly naming the governing body.

∞

Plans for the University Research Park were explained to Brookshire, Short, City Manager Veeder and county officials in early 1967. Support for roads and utilities were sought by Park President W.T. Harris. Brookshire participated in the ground-breaking a year later.

∞

Something else was occurring well beyond Charlotte's city limits—a development that would have a major impact on the city and it residents. Duke Power Company began filling Lake Norman in late 1961 with the completion of Cowans Ford Dam on the Catawba River. The filling was expected to take 18 months, but heavy spring rain in 1963 resulted in the lake being filled three months ahead of time. Soon after, local residents, including William S. "Bill" Lee, who later was to become chairman of the company, began pitching their tents along the shore. By 1993, more than 25,000 families in four counties called Lake Norman home. The lake provided another major recreational amenity to the city as it sought to grow and bring in new industries and businesses and improve the livability for existing residents.

∞

Charlotte in October 1968 was the only North Carolina city to have a sales tax. Brookshire and County Commission Chairman Jim Martin had endorsed the issue and the voters approved a referendum to allow the local sales tax.

∞

Brookshire was outspoken in his support of Vice President Hubert Humphrey in his unsuccessful bid to defeat GOP candidate Richard Nixon in 1968. Brookshire also was outspoken in criticism of Nixon, who had campaigned on a program of cutting back urban programs.

∞

Heading Charlotte's successful 1968 bid to be an All-American City were chamber President Don Denton and John Belk. The good news that Charlotte was selected came in March 1969.

∞

Brookshire did preside over the year-long bicentennial celebration, but a cold rain kept attendance to under 300 when the major event was held in December 1968. A time capsule, to be opened in 2068, was buried at the law enforcement center. Lady Bird Johnson, the first lady, visited the city in May. Charlotte had been chartered by the colonial North Carolina General Assembly November 7, 1768.

∞

Brookshire left office after having handed out 2,000 keys to the city—including one to a movie star named Ronald Reagan—and cutting many, many ribbons. His last speech blasted business leaders for their apathy in regard to City Hall and its problems.

∞

Charlotte will have another chance to review the Brookshire years when a letter he wrote in May of 1964, and buried upon the opening of the Park Road Theatres, is dug up on schedule in 2014. In his letter, Brookshire predicted a city of one million population and told of progress in urban renewal, expressway construction, annexation and racial matters.

∞

When he retired, he went back to his loves of gardening and horses and his family, including his wife, son and daughter and grandchildren. He continued to take an avid interest in city government and often wrote letters to and articles for *The Charlotte Observer* on municipal affairs.

Henry Underhill, city attorney under Brookshire and Belk and still in that position in 1994, produced a scrap of paper he got from Ann Marsh, who retired in 1993 after 33 years in City Hall. It contained Brookshire's reflections just before Christmas, 1981:

"At 76, I have reached some conclusions about life, among which are: That we should take time to smell the roses and hear the birds sing; that money isn't important above minimal requirements for comfortable living and security for old age; that giving to worthy causes, as we are able, is both a responsibility and a privilege; that serving one's fellow man is merely a partial repayment for the blessings of life; that the worth of our lives is not measured in years, but by how we use them; that recreation and pleasures are just rewards for hard work and necessary ingredients for balanced living; that family and friends become more important as we grow older; that regrets belong to the past while looking hopefully to the future; that retirement affords the opportunity to do what we want, when we want and nothing when we choose— but we are happiest when we stay busy."

Brookshire sold his business and retired in 1972 and died October 10, 1990, at the age of 85. More than 500 turned out on a cold rainy day to attend his funeral at Myers Park Methodist Church.

Part Two
John Belk 1969–1977

What Was Happening Elsewhere

1969 — Neil Armstrong first man on moon
        Charles Manson kills Sharon Tate and six others

1970 — First Earth Day held
        First women generals in military service named

1971 — William Calley convicted of murder in Mylai
        massacre
        Voting age lowered to 18
        Pentagon Papers published

1972 — Richard Nixon routs George McGovern
        Watergate break-in
        Richard Nixon goes to China

1973 — Supreme Court strikes down state limits on
        abortion
        Yom Kippur War

1974 — Richard Nixon resigns
Patty Hearst kidnapped

1975 — Vietnam War ends
Gerald Ford survives two assassination attempts

1976 — Jimmy Carter defeats Gerald Ford
National Bicentennial held
Legionnaire's disease kills 29

1977 — Jimmy Carter pardons 10,000 draft evaders
Gary Gilmore first person executed in U.S. in
10 years
Jimmy Carter cancels B-1 bomber

Chapter Nine

The Millionaire Bachelor

Mayor Stan Brookshire was only 63 in 1969, but his blonde hair was now silver and he was ready to return to his business and family. Councilman Jim Whittington, who had always coveted the mayor's chair, had almost run in 1965 and 1967 and believed it was his turn in 1969.

Lawyer Robert Lassiter Jr. was rumored to be the prime candidate to replace Brookshire as early as May 1968 and as late as January 1969, but he never made it to the filing counter. Among other things, he had been chairman of the latest committee to find a site for a downtown civic center. Lassiter, who had been captain of his Yale football team and was part of the wealthy Hanes family in Winston-Salem, seriously considered the matter but announced February 1, 1969, that he would not be a candidate. He said the demands of the mayor's office were so great that he'd have to lay aside his law practice and then have difficulty rebuilding it after leaving office.

The "downtown power structure" was stunned and it was at this point that public attention centered on

Whittington, who had been mayor pro tempore for four terms and on council for five. Conventional wisdom gave him the inside track by a wide margin for a few days despite the fact that many business leaders thought Whittington to be too rough around the edges to represent Charlotte on the national scene.

While Whittington pondered his chances, Gibson Smith did file. Smith, 55, had worked for the Belk department store chain for a quarter of a century before forming his own real estate company. He was perceived as capable and knowledgeable, but prone to be abrasive at times.

Several names were floated in the media and around town in the days following Lassiter's withdrawal. Flamboyant developer Pat Hall's and department store executive John Belk's names were prominently mentioned. Hall, then 46, said he wanted to go out of town and think about it. He and Belk huddled with media consultant Joe Epley and it was decided that Belk would be the candidate and Hall the campaign manager. Hall was just before launching his Carowinds project and was afraid that would be too time-consuming for him to also serve as mayor. Hall had such an overwhelming personality that he was told to stay behind the scenes lest he overshadow Belk. Belk, who had received a lot of public attention because of his involvement in boosting sports in the area, had flirted with the idea of running for mayor back in 1959 but didn't and James Smith was elected to his second term.

Belk, who had been courted by the likes of bankers C.C. Cameron and Addison Reese, newspaper executive Brodie Griffith, furniture executive Herbert Bridges and industrialists William H. Barnhardt and Oliver Rowe, formally announced February 21 at a news conference at the Red Carpet Inn. "We can do better," Belk said and spoke of

Charlotte entering the "sensational 70s."

Belk had a 10-point platform, which included such things as consolidation of the city and county parks and recreation functions, greater citizen involvement, building a safer city and a promise of executive know-how. Between his decision to run and his announcement he had gone skiing, to the chagrin of his political advisers, who anxiously awaited his return.

Belk was then 49, a millionaire bachelor and president of Belk Stores Services. The Belk empire included 420 stores in 17 states. It was said in 1965 that Belk actively headed more companies than any other man in the United States.

∞

The first mention of Belk in the clipping files at *The Charlotte Observer* is in a 1952 story telling of 31-year-old first lieutenant John Belk's return to Charlotte from Korea upon the death of his father.

Belk, at 6 feet 4 inches tall and 210 pounds (he had been co-captain of his Davidson basketball team and also was a 1:50 half-miler), and blessed with a constant tan and a boyish grin, had been president of the Chamber of Commerce in 1964, *The Charlotte News*' Man of the Year in 1968, chairman of the city's bicentennial committee and had led the drive to raise $350,000 for the North Carolina Symphony Orchestra.

∞

Whittington decided not to run for mayor, citing lack of adequate funds. But Albert T. Pearson and black minister George J. Leake did file. Leake and City Councilman Fred Alexander were waging a fierce behind-the-scenes battle for leadership within the black community at the time. Gibson Smith charged that "another candidate" had paid Leake to "get at me." Brookshire backed Belk. So did *The Charlotte Observer* and *The Charlotte News*.

Belk started slowly, performed abysmally on television—particularly one disastrous appearance on WBTV—and seemed unable to get a grasp of the issues. But he developed confidence as he toured shopping centers and neighborhoods and even rode in a dry cleaning truck making its rounds. As for his television experience, Epley said years later, "John blew it. I almost cried. He was not used to being a candidate and having to do his homework. He couldn't delegate someone to remember for him."

Belk's love for his city, which he called in his molasses-thick accent, "Cha-lut," was readily apparent and infectious and eventually Belk was to gain control even of the news camera. Once, while being interviewed on television, the newsperson twice asked Belk a question as the mayor just stared straight ahead. Finally, Belk, with an innocent look on his face, asked, "Are you talking to me?" Stan Kaplan, active in Charlotte broadcasting, publishing and politics over the years, said in 1993 that he advised Belk to just answer "yes" or "no" with no elaboration at television appearances. Belk followed the advice so well, Kaplan said, that the television interviewers ran out of questions before the time was up.

This author, then a city hall reporter for *The Atlanta Constitution*, visited Charlotte just before the primary to interview a wide variety of black and white leaders about the upcoming vote. I came away with the conclusion that Smith would win because I didn't think anyone could understand what Belk was trying to say. (Yet I got a nice note from Belk calling my effort "excellent . . . and well written.")

And, in fact, five years after Belk served as mayor, Kathleen Curry of *The Charlotte News* wrote in a profile on him: "But despite the brass bands and the brassy speeches for which he is remembered, the city's most powerful person remains an enigma to nearly all surrounding him. John Belk is well-known but not known well." Curry went on to quote one of Belk's associates as saying, "Nobody fully understands John Belk, or why he does things . . . "

What I didn't realize was that I had been away from Charlotte since 1965 when Belk made so many of his civic contributions. A majority of the voters were willing to vote for him, even if they didn't understand him. The public identified with Belk and saw him as human and sincere, not the standard canned politician. And in a one-on-one setting, he was relaxed and quick-witted. Belk often defused tense situations with humor. And he loved gag gifts and could laugh at himself. Yet his humor sometimes was deemed inappropriate, particularly by feminists who didn't appreciate his Old South ways of always referring to them as "ladies." He often repeated the story that "a friend once said, 'I couldn't lead a silent prayer.'"

"I don't claim to be an outstanding speaker," Belk told the voters. "I don't claim to be a politician. I am a businessman."

It was observed that Belk "is not inarticulate. It is just that his mind works at 45 RPMs and his mouth at $33^{1/3}$." Someone else said Belk "just has a hard time getting what's in his mind out of his mouth."

It was a campaign that produced several interesting confrontations. Local businessman Perrin Henderson was program chairman of the Charlotte Kiwanis Club, which met at the Central YMCA at the time. He recalled arranging for all four candidates to appear on a luncheon program. When interviewed in early 1993, Henderson said that Pearson accused Belk of selfish motives in supporting construction of the civic center and then Leake lambasted Belk unmercifully. Smith's comments were relatively mild and then Belk stood up "and like Ronald Reagan, the teflon candidate, was smooth and disarming," Henderson said.

At another campaign outing, this time on the westside, three of the candidates were peppered with question after question on why the westside got all the "negative develop-ments" and none of the "positive" ones. Finally, Leake spoke up to say that "he (while pointing to Belk) owns the land and he (pointing to Smith, who had served on council) makes the law. You choose between them." A white man was heard to mutter under his breath, "If he (Leake) was just a little less black, I'd vote for him."

The primary results gave Smith a comfortable lead over Belk, 13,590 to 11,742. Leake with 8,963 votes and Pearson with 1,895 were eliminated. Whittington led the council ticket with 24,201 votes in the primary and got 27,912 votes in the election itself.

Even though the schools were under a separate board and funded by the county, busing threatened to become an issue. It was diffused when both Belk and Smith announced opposition to busing.

The polls, formal and informal, showed Belk behind, despite the fact that former mayors Philip Van Every and Ben Douglas also backed Belk.

Leake remained publicly neutral but was supporting Belk behind the scenes. Stan Kaplan, who with his wife Sis, had been working for Leake, said in 1993 that after the primary, he got a call from Pat Hall asking for Leake's support for Belk. Kaplan said Hall was afraid Alexander could deliver the votes of older, established blacks, but not the younger group, who were in Leake's camp. And why did the Leake-Kaplan team back Belk rather than Smith? "He asked," Stan answered. And after Alexander cautiously backed Belk, the black vote shifted to Belk and he won 19,107 to 18,706. Belk's supporters said black voters identified with Belk because of his stores, which had hired them and sold them goods for decades. Also, he had been to many, many funerals in the black (and white) community, so said the analysts.

Belk also did better among white middle-income voters than he had in the primary. Most Charlotteans have forgotten that a shift of only 201 votes out of nearly 40,000 cast would have meant that Belk, who went on to serve four terms, would not have been mayor! But he was—Charlotte's 50th. One of the first things he did was decline to accept any salary for being mayor ($10,000 a year at the beginning of his tenure and $12,000 by the time he left office), nor did he take his $6,500 car allowance.

∞

When sworn in, those standing behind the big bachelor noted that he—despite having 400 stores that sold clothing—had a massive rip in his suit jacket.

∞

Belk met District Court Judge Claudia Watkins during the 1969 campaign and announced in December 1970 that he would marry her and did so in her hometown of Durham on February 20, 1971. After he met her during the campaign, what may have started as a political meeting turned into love. Even before they were married, Belk called her "Sweet Old Girl." The new Mrs. Belk had become a judge in 1968 and served as such until her term ended at the end of 1972, when she declined to run again.

∞

Mrs. Belk, as district judge, and her husband, as mayor, recognized eight teenagers whose good behavior had resulted in their being discharged from probation in April 1971.

∞

In 1971 Belk and Hall were both suggested as candidates for governor in 1972. Neither ruled himself out. Stories in the media also centered on Belk's running immediately for other higher offices.

∞

Just before the 1971 election campaign got serious, William E. "Bill" Poe, who was chairman of the school board at the time, got a call from Belk. "May I come over to your office?" the mayor asked Poe, who readily agreed, yet wondered at the urgency of Belk's request.

Belk got to Poe's office, which was then in the Cameron Brown Building, a few minutes later. The mayor looked worried and clutched a large, brown envelope tightly. "What's this all about?" Belk said, still with a worried look on his face.

Poe looked at an 8 x 10 photograph Belk pulled from the envelope. The picture showed a huge political billboard reading, "Bill Poe for Mayor." It should be noted here that some people had suggested Poe should run for mayor, but he had expressed no interest.

It was then that Poe realized that Belk was pulling another one of his practical jokes. The sign was from Tampa, Florida, where the incumbent mayor, running for reelection, was named Bill Poe.

∞

Belk announced for reelection in 1971 with his wife by his side. A key part of his announcement was a pledge to rid the city of "lewdness and obscenity." While it was speculated that a campaign issue would be the locating of the Civic Center diagonally across from the downtown Belk flagship store, Belk was opposed only by perennial candidate Albert T. Pearson and won easily 20,533 to 7,977. Leake declined to run, saying, "A face-to-face confrontation with a multi-millionaire who has made few mistakes in office is not good political savvy." Belk often stopped in for coffee at Pearson's downtown snack bar, and, once, when he offered to pay, he was told by Pearson the coffee was free and a campaign contribution.

Fred Alexander led the council ticket this time and thereby ousted Whittington as mayor pro tempore. Whittington had served 10 years as mayor pro tempore and was said by his friends to be stunned by the outcome. Jim McDuffie, sometimes considered merely a nuisance, won election to council after two failures. Leadership on council was spread between Alexander, Whittington and Milton Short.

∞

In December 1971 attorney Myles Haynes led a delegation to try to convince Poe to run for the congressional seat being vacated by Republican Charles R. Jonas of Lincolnton. Poe didn't say no, but insiders said the chances of his making the race were slim. Poe was also urged to run for the congressional seat by several other political leaders. The end result was a race between Republican County Commission Chairman Jim Martin of Davidson and Democratic State Representative Jim Beatty. Martin won.

∞

When asked in June 1973 if he intended to seek a third term later that year, Belk told reporters, "Spring is when you plant your cotton crop but then a freeze will generally come along and kill all the boll weevils. After that is when you see what the crop looks like. I'm still just planting the seeds right now."

Heavier opposition did come in 1973 after the election had been moved from the spring to the fall by action of the General Assembly. A Republican proposal to change elections from non-partisan to partisan was suggested for 1973 to help GOP Mecklenburg County Chairman and former County Commissioner Henry Wilmer, but this idea was opposed by Belk and his Democratic council colleagues and was delayed until 1975. A plan to annex 48,838 suburbanites also was delayed by the courts until after the election, thereby depriving Wilmer of an election issue.

∞

The mayor's pay had been upped $1,000 to $11,000, starting in January. Belk still turned his back in.

∞

McDuffie had been critical of Belk's involvement in site selection of the Civic Center and had even taken the matter to court. He charged that the newly opened center was a barn. On and off council, McDuffie had been a maverick and a gadfly. Belk had ignored him, tolerated him and laughed at him at first, but later had started to be impatient with him. Belk said crime was the number one issue. The Police Department was under fire at the time from various segments of the community.

When Belk filed, he did it with characteristic humor, by asking if he could use an IOU for his $200 filing fee. When he did hand over the $20 bills, he said he had taken up a collection within his family to raise the money.

Belk, who was newly married at the time of the 1971 election, announced on the eve of the 1973 election that he was to be a father for the first time. A daughter, Mary Claudia, was born at 1:58 p.m. Christmas Eve, 1973, at Presbyterian Hospital.

Belk won the primary with 7,993 votes to McDuffie's

4,325 and Socialist Labor candidate Jim Rumley's 449. Rumley was arrested just before the election for using a loudspeaker without a permit in front of the Belk store downtown. In the election itself, the vote was Belk, 26,373, and McDuffie, 17,830. Belk did well, as had Brookshire, in the black and silk stocking precincts. McDuffie got his votes in the northeast middle-income boxes. Belk's campaign theme was "to improve the quality of life for all humans," which was not precise enough for newspaper editorialists but specific enough for the voters. The newspapers also took Belk to task for not being involved in the continuing school desegregation issue, but praised County Commission Chairman W.T. Harris for speaking out in support of the school system's efforts to comply with the court order.

Belk did say at the time that the city's top problems were the school situation and housing.

∞

In January 1974, Belk was suggested as a possible successor to United States Senator Sam Ervin, who was retiring. Belk didn't say yes, but he didn't close the door immediately to the idea. Robert Morgan eventually won the office, only to lose his reelection bid to John East and the Congressional Club. And in July, Belk's name was one of several suggested as a gubernatorial candidate. Jim Hunt eventually was elected to the first of his terms as governor.

∞

With 1975 came the first partisan election with a record number of candidates filing. Belk had said he didn't favor the move to partisan voting, but he wouldn't actively fight it. The four Democratic members of City Council also favored retaining non-partisan elections, but the voters disagreed.

Belk kept everyone guessing until the last minute and then August 20 announced his candidacy for the September 23 primary. Some speculated that he might have stepped aside had former State Senator Eddie Knox, who was to become mayor in 1979, filed. But what happened was that Knox and Belk met just before the filing deadline in Pat Hall's railroad car, and when they emerged Belk was in the race and Knox was out. In answer to a reporter's question, Belk said he (Belk) "had more knowledge at this time." Sixteen years later, Belk declined to publicly criticize Knox, but it was clear Belk had strong reservations about the accomplishments of the next Democrat to hold the position after he (Belk) left office. City Council members Whittington, Short, and Joe Withrow, as well as Knox, had been suggested as Democratic candidates but Belk's probable run for a fourth term scared all of them out of the race. McDuffie was now a state senator and did file for the Democratic primary, as did David Newton, a UNC Charlotte senior.

Political scientist Schley Lyons, dean of UNC Charlotte's College of Arts and Sciences when he was interviewed in 1993, said Belk was the bridge between the old and the new politics. During Belk's last years in office, the GOP was beginning to develop a political base and was then a homogeneous group without factions. "It was a minority party with fire in the eye," he said. "It was something you couldn't ignore . . . and a lot of whites were making the transition (from the Democratic to the Republican Party)." This meant that Belk had to worry about the possibility of losing to a Republican, Lyons said, thus the black vote, which traditionally was almost solidly Democratic, was even more important to him.

Belk ousted McDuffie and Newton in the primary by

gathering 9,915 votes to McDuffie's 6,621 and Newton's 331. Rain and voter apathy kept the vote down in the middle-income precincts where McDuffie had his strength, and Belk, as usual, did well in the black and the silk stocking precincts. For example, he got 79 percent of the vote in the upper income boxes and 86 percent in the black boxes. Hank Wilmer defeated James R. Warner and Herb Neubauer in the GOP primary and Mark Englander beat Stanley Ezrol in the Labor Party primary.

Asked about the rising neighborhood movement that threatened the way city government had been run for decades, Belk answered, "I grew up in a neighborhood. I think neighborhoods are the best thing you can have." Belk touted the move of the city's bond rating from AA to AAA and added that the city had had no tax increase in four years. The improvement in the credit rating saved the city millions of dollars through the years and made possible many of the civic improvements at lower interest rates. Belk also noted that 16 new neighborhood parks had been created and that 400 miles of street improvements had been made.

In the general election, Belk got 19,940 votes with Wilmer getting 16,906 and Englander getting 916. This time Belk and Wilmer more or less divided the upper income vote, but the black vote gave Belk his fourth term. For example, Belk got 505 votes while Wilmer got 62 in the West Charlotte High School Precinct and had a 4,053 (more than his overall margin) edge in predominantly black precincts. The Black Political Caucus had backed Belk. Fred Alexander, who by then had moved from the City Council to the State Senate, was credited with being Belk's biggest booster in the black community. Belk carried only 39 precincts overall, while Wilmer carried 42 across the city.

Belk said after the election that it was probably the last time a mayor would be elected by "old Charlotte." Other observers noted that many newcomers to Charlotte were more concerned with their neighborhoods and tax bills than with such catalysts to development as the Civic Center or airport.

Lyons said that Belk presided over the city during turbulent times from political, social and economic standpoints and may or may not have fully understood "what he was astride" as blacks, women and newcomers to the city sought to get a greater piece of the pie. The irony was that Brookshire's and Belk's programs that sparked economic development brought in newcomers that changed the "old Charlotte" that they and their contemporaries felt so comfortable with. "Belk helped unleash forces that became uncontrollable," he said. "Later, district representation was to make the GOP a full partner and also help blacks," Lyons said.

Whittington led the council ticket again and thereby was selected mayor pro tempore. He received almost 1,000 more votes than Belk. Harvey Gantt surprised some observers by finishing second in his first election bid and Betty Chafin, who was to have a major impact on politics for several years afterward, was also elected to council for the first time.

∞

District representation came again in April 1977— Charlotte had had district representation in 1851–1917 and 1929–45—and some said that had a bearing on Belk's decision not to seek a fifth term. When interviewed for this book in 1993, Richard Vinroot, then mayor of Charlotte, said Belk "didn't fight district representation, but he didn't embrace it either." But because the elections had been shifted from the spring to the fall during his tenure, Belk became the longest-serving mayor in the city's history—eight-and-a-half years to Brookshire's eight years.

∞

By January of 1977, prognosticators were seeing possible mayoral candidates such as Belk, Gantt, Knox, Whittington, lawyer Tom Ray, Short and McDuffie among the Democrats and Wilmer, insurance man Ken Harris, council members Pat Locke and Neil Williams and former Democrat-turned-Republican Councilman Don Bryant among the Republicans. Short said in 1993 that he never seriously contemplated running for mayor because he saw the negative impact being mayor had on Herb Baxter (1943–49) in terms of the time required away from business for ceremonial duties. Knox said he had promised Whittington he wouldn't run against him and dropped out. Knox said later he advised Whittington that time had passed him by and he shouldn't run, but Whittington ran anyway. Whittington said his memory is that Knox sent his brother Charles to try to keep Whittington out of the race so Eddie could run.

Speculation continued through the summer while Belk kept his plans to himself. When someone in Washington asked him if he planned to run, Belk said he might retire for health reasons. The questioner was alarmed and asked, "Well, are you sick?" "No," the mayor quipped, "the folks back home may be sick of me." A month before the filing deadline of August 26, he said he would not run again. Pat Hall mulled a run, but didn't file.

Brookshire called on former School Board Chairman Bill Poe and pleaded with him to offer his candidacy. Poe gave Brookshire's suggestion serious consideration. But, Poe said, 16 years later, he backed out because he wanted to spend more time with his large family and with his law practice. Poe said that the following years were very profitable and he was confident he made the right decision.

Belk backed Whittington, the Democratic nominee, but Brookshire backed Harris, the Republican. Harris was to say in later years that he considered Brookshire one of his mentors and conferred with him often after he became mayor. "I could rely on him to give me the real truth," Harris said. Belk waited until just before the election to endorse Whittington and some political analysts suggested this kept some uptown business money from going Whittington's way.

Harris won.

Years later, former County Commission Chairman Charles M. Lowe lamented that Whittington had never achieved the goal he so dearly cherished. Lowe blamed the news media for its portrayal of Whittington. "Everyone has a dream and they (the media) spit on his dream."

∞

As he stepped down, Belk received accolade after accolade and it was said in newspaper editorials that he sought office "out of a sense of duty, not ambition" and that he almost always showed "good will, affection and good humor" while serving. Newspapers across the South took note not only of the end of the Belk administration but also of the end of the businessman-as-mayor era.

As he left office, he credited his father with being the greatest influence in his life and named Duke Power Company's role in providing energy to the area as being the single most significant factor in Charlotte's success.

∞

Belinda Crowell, who worked for Belk throughout his time in City Hall and was administrative assistant to Mayor

Richard Vinroot in 1994, produced Belk's prepared statement upon his announcement that he would not seek
another term:

"For the past eight years I have served the people of
Charlotte as their mayor. I wish I were capable of expressing
in words my feeling of solemn pride at having been so
honored and trusted. Charlotte has been good to me and it
will be my eternal hope to be remembered as someone who
was good to Charlotte.

"Charlotte is much more than vast areas of residences
and towering buildings. The greatest asset of Charlotte by
far is its good people. To realize the best in a government of
the people, it is essential that there be a variety of leadership.
Therefore, with a feeling that is hard for me to put into
words, I wish to pass the office of mayor to another of your
choosing. I hereby state that I shall not be a candidate for
office in the upcoming city election.

"I shall always do whatever I can to help make Charlotte
one of the best places in the land, and to that end shall
always offer the best hopes of my mind, my heart and my
soul."

∞

When he came into office, the city had 240,000 citizens
within 73 square miles. When he left, it had 320,000 in 124
square miles. The Convention Center and the Northwestern, First Union, NCNB, Wachovia and Southern National
bank towers as well as the Overstreet, SouthPark and
Eastland malls, plus development of Marshall Park, Discovery Place and Spirit Square were other testaments to his
leadership. It was said that he would have accomplished
even more had not the courts bottled up development of the
expressway system, First Ward redevelopment and the new
airport.

Chapter Ten

The People and How They Got Along . . . or Didn't

Mayor Belk was often praised for not worrying about who got credit for successes in city government. He was said to be spending 90 hours a week on city and private business soon after he took office. Belk said he spent about 40 on city business, usually including two hours a day at City Hall. He was the last Charlotte mayor who did not keep regular office hours at City Hall. But the staff would set up appointments with constituents and he would show up. His secretary Carol Cannon kept track of four calendars for Belk—one for city business, one for the Belk mercantile business, one for other outside business and, in 1974, one for business of the National Retail Merchants Association of which Belk was chairman. One thing veteran television newsman Doug Mayes recalled about Belk years later was how organized he was. Belk told Mayes it was because of the daily schedule of events and meetings he carried on a small card in his pocket.

∞

It was said that it seemed very difficult to make him angry and that he showed amazing courtesy in the exercise of his public duties. Yet one city employee confessed years later to be scared to death of Belk "because I couldn't understand him. I was beside myself. I never knew what he wanted." Belk did get impatient and angry at times because city government didn't respond as quickly to his suggestions and ideas as did his private business. And he had a hard time understanding people who didn't love his city as much as he did. Former veteran City Councilman Jim Whittington said, "No one loved Charlotte more . . . He saw himself as the quarterback and council members as the linemen . . ." Whittington contended that Belk's relationship with city council members was closer than that of any other mayor. Yet Belk was known to cut off critics—elected and non-elected—at council meetings from time to time. One veteran city employee, who worked throughout Brookshire's and Belk's terms, said that Belk "wasn't courtly like Brookshire, but he was gracious nonetheless."

Liz Hair, who served on the Mecklenburg County Commission from 1972 to 1980 and chaired it for three years, remembered Belk's courteousness and thoughtfulness more than anything else. She said she once was on crutches because of a sprained ankle and Belk came to her house for an early morning meeting rather than force her to have to go out. "I never saw him be discourteous," she said years later. Nor did Hair remember any contentious disagreements between the two.

Susan Jetton, who covered City Hall for *The Charlotte Observer* during the 1970s and in 1993 was a speech writer for the governor of Louisiana, also vouched for Belk's thoughtfulness with this story:

Belk was host to the mayors of North Carolina's largest

cities at a gathering at Quail Hollow Country Club. The mayors were to play golf in the morning, have lunch together and then meet for discussions in the afternoon. When Jetton arrived at Quail Hollow, she was shown into the room where the lunch was to be held, only to then be told she couldn't remain because it was the men's locker room. About this time, Belk strode in, asked what the problem was and then ordered the luncheon tables to be set up in the dining area—where Jetton could join the group.

Once Belk endured a particularly harsh diatribe from a citizen during a council meeting and then council broke for a recess. The disturbed citizen lay in wait for Belk, who, upon reaching the place where the man stood, said, "Are you still cheating at cards?" and walked on past into the mayor's office. That rendered the man defenseless, Belk said, as his friends started querying him about his card-playing habits.

Someone asked a top city official how it was to work for a millionaire mayor. The city staffer said it wasn't any different than working for other less affluent officials, except that Belk had the "privilege of always saying what he thinks. And it worked for the good of the city, even though it got him in trouble sometimes."

Jetton said when interviewed for this book that while she "always liked the mayor very much . . . and his major strength was finding good people, putting them in the right slot and letting them work, his weaknesses were never understanding he couldn't run the city like he ran his stores . . . and that he never understood what it was like to live from one pay check to another."

Bill Guerrant, who ran the city's public service and information department through most of Belk's administration and into the 1990s, said that Belk "was one of the most unusual people I ever worked for. Because of his family and status, some may have thought he was aloof or cold. But he was the kindest, most caring person I knew. He always asked how your family was doing and how you liked your job. He'd compliment the staff and always had a little joke . . . The punch line didn't always make sense but it made you laugh anyway. It took me eight years to understand him and maybe I didn't fully understand him then. I still call him mayor. He was a mayor in the truest sense," Guerrant said.

Former City Manager Bill Veeder called Belk "a very good leader of council. He very seldom lost his cool. If so, he did it privately." Veeder noted later that Belk "has done a helluva lot for the city that people don't know about . . . He is devoted to Charlotte . . . and was not motivated by personal gain or to use the mayor's office as a stepping stone, but, just simply—I know it sounds corny—because he loved Charlotte."

∞

"He (Belk) didn't understand people who were critical of Charlotte," said Jetton. "He took it personally because he was so intertwined with the city. (In his mind) he and Charlotte were the same thing." Veteran newsman Doug Mayes said he always thought Belk believed "what's good for Charlotte is good for John Belk."

Bill Carstarphen, Veeder's assistant for several years and Greensboro's city manager in 1994, said the same thing—"The greatest thing about John Belk was his unabashed love for Charlotte . . . He was not the reserved elder statesman (that Brookshire was), but just as friendly and sincere with his staff and with people. He was strong willed when he had to be. My overwhelming impression of him was his friendliness."

Veeder said Belk had an amazing capacity "to analyze and act, to come to a conclusion . . . and sometimes be the first one to figure it out."

Milton Short, who served on the City Council for all but two years between 1965 and 1979, put it simply: "John is the finest mayor we've ever had."

Short said that Belk as mayor was "one of the most effective people you're ever likely to see in a leadership role. And his weaknesses contributed to his leadership." Short explained that by saying that even when Belk's thoughts and tongue got tangled up, it contributed to his leadership by making him more human and likable. "And when (City Manager) Burkhalter planted an idea with Belk, he was talking to a man who could get it done as well as anyone I've ever seen."

Guerrant said it a different way: "Belk had the vision and in his quiet way Burkhalter accomplished things (to achieve the vision)."

Burkhalter said when Belk proposed something or responded to something, he always asked, "What's in the best interests of the city?"—not how would it look.

∞

Former television newsman Joe Epley, who worked in each of Belk's election campaigns, said Belk was the only Charlotte mayor to "have national clout." Others turned their thoughts inside to the city. Belk focused toward the national scene, Epley noted during an interview for this book.

City Attorney Henry Underhill, who served in that position from Brookshire's administration through the writing of this book, recalled one episode that illustrates Epley's point. Underhill said he was accompanying Belk on a trip to Washington on city business. As they arrived and were walking through Washington National Airport, Underhill spied George McGovern, the liberal Democratic senator from South Dakota. McGovern waved and hailed Belk by name. Later in the day, as Belk and Underhill were leaving and on their way back to Charlotte, they were again in Washington National Airport and this time they saw Jesse Helms, the conservative senator from North Carolina. Helms' greeting was just as warm as McGovern's, Underhill recalled.

Executive search firm owner Jim Beatty, who served in the North Carolina House in 1966–72, traveled across the nation as a guest commentator on ABC's Wide World of Sports during much of Belk's tenure. He said he often ran into sports people who said, "Yes, I know Charlotte. Isn't your mayor a Belk?"

"He could bring to the table a great deal of power and influence," said Guerrant, "yet you almost didn't know what was happening . . . because of his genteel manner. It's a thing that's dying away these days. He raised the prominence of the mayor's position to a new plateau."

Former Mayor Eddie Knox, who served in City Hall in 1979–83, admitted that Belk could command more "credence" in certain national circles than he. "Guys with dollars bring more prestige because of who they are," he said. "A Belk goes farther than a Knox." Newspaper publisher Rolfe Neill, when interviewed for this book, also made the point that Belk was well connected all across the country.

Former County Commission Chairman Charles M. Lowe said when interviewed that it is rare that a man with as much money as Belk was willing to put himself in a position where he would draw as much "abuse and trouble. That's the mark of a real man . . . It would have been easy for him to be a Republican, but he had great respect for his fellow man . . . He believed in living most and serving best . . . He has done more in giving his money, time and talent for the community than any other man I know . . . He knew more things about more people than anyone in North Carolina," said Lowe, a staunch Democrat.

∞

Lowe went on to say he believed the difference between Democrats and Republicans is that Democrats are for people and Republicans are for things. If Democrats see something that makes sense for people, they are for it. If Republicans see something that makes sense dollarwise, they are for it. "It's the difference between the heart and the mind. You've got to find the point where they cross. Then you are not cold-blooded or giving away everything you can tax people for," Lowe said.

∞

Former Councilman and Mayor Harvey Gantt said in an interview for this book that when he joined the council in 1974 he was amazed at how fast council went through its bulky agenda. He soon realized that most of the decisions had already been made and that Belk exercised a "rather autocratic style" in presiding. Gantt believed that Belk usually did listen to citizens who came before council, but sometimes didn't. And because of his method of speaking, some citizens left "unfulfilled," Gantt said.

Belk, on the other hand, said Gantt and Milton Short talked so much on every topic that council decided it had to set up rules to limit unnecessary discussion.

Gantt said that he thought Belk was much more effective as a leader during sessions in his office than in the open council meeting. "He was very good at twisting arms— gently," he said.

Lowe said that in thinking of Belk—and Brookshire—he was reminded of the saying that if "you have a dollar and I have a dollar and we swap, we still just have a dollar. But if we both have an idea and swap ideas, we then have two ideas." Belk and Brookshire were good about cooperating with other officials without insisting on always winning, Lowe observed.

∞

In early 1972 *The Charlotte Observer* good-naturedly tweaked Belk for his "sly razzle-dazzle" method of speaking. The *Observer* offered examples of Belk's style and wondered in print whether Belk meant to confuse or was really confused.

Two of the examples dealt with an appointment, about which Belk said, "I'm not sure of the numerical number (to be appointed)," and later added, "I don't think it (the appointment) will necessarily be male or female."

∞

Not only could Belk bring a laugh with his comments, his actions also were entertaining. Once while on his way back from a New Orleans meeting and due back in Charlotte for a City Council meeting the next day, bad weather forced a plane cancellation in Atlanta. He and his traveling companions, Councilman Fred Alexander and newspaper executive Brodie Griffith hired a taxi to bring them the last leg of the trip. About halfway, the taxicab driver grew sleepy, so the mayor-department store magnate took over and drove the cab back to Charlotte.

∞

Throughout his political life—and actually before and after it, Belk had as many non sequiturs attributed to him as Yogi Berra. Belk had "an uncanny inability to express himself," one friend said.

But did he? Belk said he once got two bits of solid advice from Bishop Herbert Spaugh, who spent a great deal of time in the public eye as chairman of the Charlotte Board of Education. Spaugh told Belk to remember that 1) he was no smarter after getting elected to public office than he had been before and 2) when someone makes you mad, think of the funniest thing you can and say it. It will relax you and shake up your critics, Spaugh told Belk. Belk was a master at following Spaugh's advice.

And many of Belk's comments end up sounding like wisdom once considered a second or third time.

For example, he was quoted as saying:

"I can see the cloud in the distance and want to make sure I'm near the hen house."

"We ought to decide where our problems are and implement our own."

"Public officials live in a glass house and must appear at the front door. And you have to be dressed right."

"I think you are getting into something you don't want to get out of."

"Sometimes I get so far out in left field I run out of grass." And, "Sometimes I'm out in left field and we're on the basketball court."

"You don't have to confuse me because I don't know enough about it to be confused."

"Tell us what it is and we'll know whether we didn't get it or not."

"You can't be unreasonable about something until you get the facts."

"Some people drink from the fountain of knowledge. Others just gargle."

Once, in introducing Hubert Humphrey in Charlotte, he forgot the vice president's first name and referred to him as "Honorable Humphrey." Humphrey assumed it was a joke and thanked "Honorable Belk."

And, Carstarphen recalled later, Belk once explained that "when you have a progress in your problem, that's a good thing because you can do something about it."

And finally, Belk once admitted, "I get a little mixed up when I stop and think."

∞

But Belk always got the last laugh because he constantly won at the ballot box and, surprise, surprise, in mid-1974, the North Carolina Chapter of the International Association of Business Communicators gave him its Communicator of the Year Award!

∞

Former County Commission Chairman Lowe in 1993 recalled the time he and Belk went to a rural church, where Belk was to make a speech. Upon arriving, Belk was surprised to see several mothers breast-feeding their babies on the front row. Belk's mouth dropped open and he said he couldn't go through with his speech, so Lowe said, "I gave his speech for him." When the collection plate was passed, Lowe told Belk he didn't have any money. Belk put in $20 for Lowe. Later, whenever Belk called Lowe to remind him that Lowe owed him $20, Lowe would jest that that was his fee for making Belk's speech for him.

∞

Belinda Crowell, who served as Belk's secretary throughout his four terms, said that she had been prepared for Belk's method of communicating when she arrived from the old water department. "I had been told that he was difficult to communicate with but easy to work with . . . But it didn't take long to know what he was saying . . . And he was very generous and enjoyed the people in the office, professionally and socially."

As for Belk, he once said after stopping by to visit with Crowell's family, "Belinda's her mother's apple."

∞

Belk was almost always in control and few challenged him—because of his physical size, wealth and position. But he did get his comeuppance at least three times:

• When Belk and Ivey's held a "bridge party" to open the new walkway over Tryon between the two department stores in late 1978, Belk's five-year-old daughter Mary Claudia was on hand. Belk asked her if she wanted some "of Daddy's cake or some of George's." She pointed out the cake of George Ivey Jr. as her choice.

• Belk told the story on himself of the time he was playing golf at Charlotte Country Club and not doing particularly well, even for him. At one point, Belk observed to his caddy, who didn't know Belk from Arnold Palmer, "I bet I'm the worst golfer at Charlotte Country Club!" "No, sir," the caddy said, "they all say John Belk is the worst player out here."

• Former British Prime Minister Margaret Thatcher was speaking at the Quail Hollow Country Club to the Charlotte Foreign Policy Forum and Belk was the master of ceremonies. After her speech, she went into a question-and-answer period. Belk apparently thought the session had gone on long enough and he stood up to indicate time was up. Thatcher turned toward Belk, and snapped, "You sit down." He did.

∞

Charlotte was changing rapidly throughout the Belk years and not just physically. Earlier mayors had had a coterie of downtown power types to back them on major issues, but all this was changing by 1972. Younger leaders had arisen, but didn't have the magic to their names as had Ed Burnside, Paul Younts and others of that ilk.

Knox said that Brookshire and Belk operated in entirely different atmospheres than he did. He said the power they had came from their being a part of "old Charlotte" and they had a cohesive group of council members to work with. "Council members were white Anglo-Saxon males. It took a different kind of leadership (to lead council later). Council members (under Brookshire and Belk) didn't have as many agendas (of their own) as later," Knox said. Knox, on the other hand, said he had to deal with a much more diverse council such as with council members Minette Trosch and Harvey Gantt. "Give me a (W.T.) Harris, a (Charlie) Lowe and a (Pat) Hall and I could go a long way with them." Knox contended that the so-called "old Charlotte" power structure could win 90 percent of the time in the past, yet only about 40 percent of the time in the 1990s.

Sue Myrick, Charlotte's mayor in 1987–91, said that Belk went into office "with a lot of stature . . . John was a legend . . . He was a bigger-than-life figure. He was blunt in some of his statements and some people thought they were stupid. Later, they realized why he said what he did."

Myrick also agreed with Knox that it was easier to get things done in City Hall in the Brookshire-Belk days than later on when "the good old boy system" no longer existed. "They decided something and carried it out. No matter if someone opposed them. It was tough luck. It happened anyway," she said. No matter what you thought about the system, it was a fact of life that changed with district representation, she said.

Ken Harris, the Republican mayor who served two years between Belk and Knox, agreed that city government changed dramatically from the "old boy" style enjoyed by

Brookshire and Belk, but charged in 1993 that Knox "politicized" city government "and we haven't recovered yet." Harris said he approached the mayor's job as a civic responsibility, just as Brookshire and Belk had, but discovered he couldn't take the required time away from his businesses. So he stepped down after two years. He confessed he was for district representation and worked behind the scenes to achieve it.

In addition, interests and demands of newcomers and newly organized groups had to be balanced with those of traditional groups. Gantt, a council member under Belk, Harris, and Knox, and mayor in 1983–87, said he considered such mayors as Brookshire and Belk "as extensions of the Chamber of Commerce, and believed essentially that what was good for business was good for Charlotte." As the city became more cosmopolitan and diverse, Gantt said, all did not always agree with that premise. In a sense, Gantt added, Brookshire, Belk and their kind became "victims of their own success" because a thriving Charlotte attracted newcomers who wanted a greater voice in city affairs than had Charlotteans of a previous era.

Actually, Gantt said, "they (Brookshire and Belk) were right for their time . . . but things started to break up when all these other voices in the city wanted to have a say . . . Growth for growth's sake got a closer look from the new constituents." Gantt said he greatly admired Belk's commitment and love for the city and that Belk's determination to promote planning and transportation so the city would be able to accommodate the coming growth "made sense then . . . Yet he had a vision that was not always shared by everyone else."

Jonathan Yardley, in his 1971 review of a book by former Atlanta Mayor Ivan Allen Jr. on his years as mayor, said similar things: "Mr. Allen's is, of course, the all-too-familiar attitude of American business. A genuinely public-spirited and able man, he is nonetheless unable to perceive that what's good for business is not necessarily good for everyone else."

∞

Ironically, Belk broke the tie on council that allowed Gantt to join the council on the resignation of a member. "I was glad he let me have the chance to find out how much I liked politics," Gantt said. Years later, Belk said he liked to kid Gantt about being responsible for starting Gantt off in politics. "And I told him he was educated beyond his abilities," Belk said.

∞

Stan Kaplan, who has been active in broadcasting, publishing, and politics in Charlotte for many years, said when interviewed that Belk was "the last overwhelmingly strong mayor who could make policy all by himself." Sis Kaplan, his wife who also has been active in the same business, civic and political circles, said that she could think of no one throughout the history of the city (except perhaps NationsBank's chairman Hugh McColl) who ever had as much strength and influence. Her husband chimed in to say that the irony was that Belk might have had as much and maybe even more power before he was elected as after. Stan went on to say that "Belk has never been in a fair fight—because of his background, his money, his position and his community standing. And that's not true of McColl, because he has to deal with bankers of equal weight."

Richard Vinroot, mayor of Charlotte in 1994, agreed that Brookshire and Belk governed in an entirely different time than their successors. Belk had "great economic clout, second to none," Vinroot said. Because of the changing times, Vinroot questioned whether the two would have been as effective in the 1980s and 1990s as in the 1960s and 1970s. He said that Belk continued to take an avid interest in the city into the 1990s "and I got a note from him recently about a matter; in fact, one we disagree about. But he was, as he always is, gracious about it."

Vinroot said that Brookshire and Belk did leave footprints within city government "and I am proud to walk in them and try to fill them." He said he found it interesting that when he ran into an elderly man from Alabama at a municipal seminar in Atlanta, the man asked about that "wonderful Belk boy."

Former City Councilman John Thrower served two terms under Brookshire and one under Belk and said he considered Belk "the best mayor we ever had and ever will have." Thrower, like many others, noted that while "the ideas were in there, when they came out they weren't necessarily in order."

∞

A major event occurred in August 1973 when David Burkhalter, who had succeeded Veeder as city manager in May 1971, attacked the Chamber of Commerce (obviously with Belk's knowledge and approval) for issuing opinions and reports, specifically on transportation, without having given sufficient study to them. Belk also said the chamber had abdicated its responsibilities during the school desegregation struggle. The chamber's last pronouncement on the matter had been in February 1970 when it expressed confidence in the school board.

On the other hand, Carstarphen said he believed that Belk was instrumental in getting the chamber and city government to work better together after a period of knocking heads and "circling each other suspiciously."

Yet one newspaper reporter wrote in the mid-1970s that the "romance" that once existed between the downtown power structure and City Hall was over.

Nevertheless, Belk still could count on most of Charlotte's business leaders to support him and his campaign to run Charlotte like a business. Most of these leaders were in the Downtown (officially, the Charlotte) Rotary Club, of which Belk was a member and which served as a forum and gathering place to drum up the support Belk needed. One city official called it an "oligarchy . . . The socially elite ran Charlotte."

Charlotte Observer reporter Jetton wrote in March 1975 that City Hall was opening up and the "Father Knows Best" and noblesse oblige ways of doing things in the past were becoming passé. She cited an example from two years before when the city officials hoped to ease through the York Road landfill proposal without stirring up the public, but *The Charlotte Observer* and neighborhood groups forced a full airing of the issue.

Jetton admitted that the city was indeed lucky to have the professionalism of city staff, which then presided over a $70.5 million budget and 3,555 employees.

In May of the same year, *The Charlotte Observer*'s Jerry Shinn wrote that the business establishment, which got such things as the Coliseum, Ovens Auditorium, Civic Center and airport built and the local sales tax passed, had wooed the city's heart like an "ardent, sometimes arrogant, mostly faithful lover . . . "

That day was passing, Shinn wrote, and Belk suggested it was all part of a nationwide anti-business climate. The end of joint Chamber of Commerce-City Hall decisions that were automatically implemented probably started in 1973 when 10 of 13 bond issue items failed and continued when the voters rejected a $55 million airport bond package in the spring of 1975.

Banker Luther Hodges Jr., who was the incoming chairman of the Chamber of Commerce, said that the chamber could still exert leadership, but the rising tide of populism and consumerism meant that its influence was reduced. Broadcaster Stan Kaplan noted that while the old power structure had done positive things, it never was "black, young, female or middle income . . . " Those interviewed by Shinn blamed the news media for giving anti-establishment voices more credibility and importance than they deserved.

Veeder, who by then had left City Hall, told *The Charlotte Observer* that city officials might better start in the neighborhoods with their programs and let the citizens react before putting the plans together. "It is time consuming and maybe frustrating and sometimes it might be a complete waste of time," he admitted. District representation and new mechanisms for citizen participation were looming, he indicated. Ironically, Veeder always had been known for operating very close to the vest within a relatively closed system when he was in city government.

∞

Belk and Burkhalter worked well together, very similarly to the way Brookshire and Veeder had worked. And clippings show that whenever Belk was interviewed, Burkhalter was inevitably at his side. Burkhalter remained at City Hall through Belk's time there and retired in 1981 during Eddie Knox's tenure. Former Councilman Short, when interviewed for this book, was high in his praise for Burkhalter, but then explained some differences between him and his predecessor, Veeder. "He (Burkhalter) is a very attractive gentleman, soft-spoken. Veeder is profane, a man's man. Their methods were different." Short said that Veeder would challenge his bosses on council, something Burkhalter would never do. "He was a helluva task master," one person who worked closely with Veeder said years later. "He told you what he wanted and chewed you out if you didn't do it." This same person said that Burkhalter's "gregarious, nice guy approach" and Belk's unique way of phrasing things resulted in there being "a lot of puzzled people around City Hall" for a time.

"I loved that man," *The Charlotte Observer's* Jetton said of Burkhalter in 1993. "David could disarm with a word any citizen, reporter, councilman—or mayor . . . He was an outstanding politician—maybe the best politician of the bunch—and he knew how to work John Belk. They had a good relationship and, like the mayor, he hired good people."

∞

After Veeder left in January 1971, former Assistant City Manager Paul Bobo was named acting city manager. He had been at Veeder's side for 10 years. Many City Hall insiders thought Bobo would get the top job and, in fact, he went into the last weekend in March as the favorite. Councilmen Whittington, Thrower and Sandy Jordan favored him, while Councilmen Short, Alexander and Joe Withrow were behind Carstarphen, the other assistant city manager. Belk leaned toward Carstarphen, but would have a vote only in case of a tie. Councilman Jerry Tuttle leaned toward Bobo. At least, that's what the news media reported. But by Sunday, council apparently decided not to risk an open fight and went outside the local city government to name Burkhalter, 59, of Springfield, Missouri, to the $31,500 post. Burkhalter was the immediate past president of the International City Manager's Association.

Jordan was not happy with the decision nor with being

left out of at least part of the decision-making process. With his council colleagues and Bobo looking on embarrassed, Jordan blasted them for the Burkhalter selection.

∞

Belinda Crowell recalled Burkhalter's first day at City Hall, more than 20 years later. She said he came into the office just outside the mayor's and manager's office, stepped up onto a secretary's desk, stepped back down and strode on into his own office. Why? "I don't know," Crowell said, "He just did funny things." Burkhalter remembered the incident less dramatically and said he recalled just faking the step up on the desk because the space between two desks was jammed with people. But, he said good-naturedly, "My memory is also self serving." The desk in question belonged to Paulette Purgason, who subsequently was in charge of public information at the airport. She laughed about the matter more than 20 years later and said the City Hall staff had just been talking about "the wily old fox," as Burkhalter was referred to, when he strode in and "walked across my desk."

∞

City Attorney Henry Underhill agreed that Veeder's and Burkhalter's management styles "were completely different. Burkhalter spent time warming up . . . with light conversation to put you at ease . . . It was often difficult to know the purpose of the meeting at first . . . I'm not being critical. It was just his style. He was the warmest, friendliest man and I enjoyed working for him . . . But he did seem to have a difficult time making decisions. He seemed to want to put them off. Veeder just made decisions and lived with them."

Guerrant said Burkhalter's style was what was needed for the time. His first description was "grandfatherly." He added that it was "solid . . . and quiet. Some said too quiet, but I don't think so."

Guerrant contended that Burkhalter had to deal with few really difficult issues. Unlike later, when dollars were very short, Burkhalter's time in City Hall was marked by a period when "a lot of money was available . . . The city was in a growth mode. We had a lot of bond issues and built a lot of roads."

Whittington said when interviewed that Burkhalter and Belk were indeed very close and he (Whittington) credited Burkhalter with bringing a great deal of innovation to city government. But another former council member, who asked not to be identified, said Burkhalter sometimes told council only what he wanted them to hear and did not offer all the options available.

Betty Chafin Rash, who served three terms on City Council, observed years later that during her first meetings with Burkhalter, the city manager "treated me like a daughter or a niece. I'd try to ask him about things like water and sewer issues and he'd tell me a story . . . But I think he learned to respect me."

Jack Bullard, who was then and in 1994 executive director of the Community Relations Committee, recalled the time when Burkhalter, ever smiling, faced a situation in which a director of a city department was not as advanced in his outlook on race as his colleagues and did not want to present a certain progressive recommendation from his department to the City Council. "I see you have some doubts," Burkhalter said, "and I'll not ask you to do it if you don't want to. But I think I can get a director who will." Bullard said Burkhalter was solidly behind the committee's efforts to help the city move in the right direction on racial matters.

Former Mayor Harris recalled that Burkhalter was a master at "lowering tension in a room . . . by telling a joke." Carstarphen said city staffers eventually learned that Burkhalter's stories usually "had a purpose or a lesson in them."

"Burkhalter was a master politician, and I say that with admiration," *Charlotte Observer* Publisher Rolfe Neill said in 1993. "He kept everybody happy and in his quiet way, he was effective and soothing. He also kept up well on what was going on (in city government)."

"Burkhalter got what he wanted, but not directly (in contrast to his predecessor Veeder)," one city official of that era said. "When I met with him, nothing seemed to happen. He let you try things."

City Council members grumbled privately that Belk and Burkhalter were setting policy and the council members were left with merely reacting. One former councilman years later said Belk ran the city government like "a benevolent dictator—and that ain't all that bad."

It was said at the time that Burkhalter ran city government like a father would run a family business.

Former Mayor Gantt said when interviewed that he was impressed by the outstanding staff Burkhalter hired. Although he said Burkhalter was greatly influenced by Belk, he was fair in his dealings with council members.

City Attorney Underhill praised Burkhalter for his wisdom in knowing when to step down. "He retired gracefully . . . " as district representation was ushered in. "He probably was not the right type of manager for an activist council. He was highly regarded and had he stayed around, he might have eroded that respect," Underhill said.

∞

After the 1973 election, Belk opposed a proposal by

Councilman Milton Short and the first Republican council members elected in recent times to the establishment of council committees. Belk called the idea "absurd" and said it would wreck the efficient professional way city business was conducted. Short was said to have ambitions for the mayor's chair, although he denied it 20 years later.

∞

Former City Councilman and Mayor Ken Harris was elected to council in 1973 with fellow Republicans Pat Locke and Neil Williams, even though the city still had non-partisan elections. He said 20 years later that he believed Belk viewed him as "a threat because I challenged the things he said . . . There was some tension, yet we were always friendly. There was no animosity. I had no ambitions for mayor at that time." Harris said that "some, mainly chamber people, I saw at the City Club were asking me why I was challenging John." Harris noted that on virtually every issue Belk had four Democratic votes to back him, so questions from the three Republicans were generally moot.

Harris praised Belk "for taking a lot of hits" on various issues. "He really believed in Charlotte!" Harris said one of Belk's greatest achievements was cleaning up the uptown area and Harris specifically mentioned making Third and Fourth one-way streets, thereby making the uptown area more accessible. Harris said it might sound minor now, but many persons at the time questioned why so many lanes were needed.

∞

Belk showed his impatience with council members in January 1974 after they split along political party lines over buying 10 garbage truck bodies. Rebidding cost $600, but Belk said the 4-3 rejection was "asinine" and council ought to take the advice of the professional staff.

Belk and Burkhalter believed that "doing it right was the best way and ultimately the cheapest way." Just as in business, they sought to implement maintenance schedules and an organized, efficient way of doing business. While this set well theoretically with everyone, citizens sometimes expected special treatment—and that's why they call it politics.

Belk suggested a 40-member task force of businessmen be named to review the 1976–77 budget of $116.6 million.

∞

Belk said in January 1975 that the city's biggest problems at that time originated with federal laws and rulings. Many projects, particularly highways and expressways, had been held up because of interpretations of federal laws on environmental impact. Federal District Court Judge James McMillan over the years presided over 31 cases against the city and held up work at the airport, urban renewal areas, expressways and other projects, Belk said.

∞

By mid-1975 City Hall observers said the council was passive, not just because of the power of Belk and Burkhalter, but because council members had abdicated their proper roles. After the 1975 election with Betty Chafin (now Betty Chafin Rash) and Lou Davis as new members and with Neil Williams and Gantt feeling more comfortable, the ways council worked changed dramatically. Whittington, who usually led by letting everyone else speak and then showing his hand, took a larger role in leading from the start.

Davis never got along well with Belk or Burkhalter and publicly criticized the city manager in March 1977. Davis' method of questioning Belk was new. Heretofore, mayors had never been as sharply challenged in public as was Davis' manner with Belk. Newspaper reporters said Davis apparently was seen as not working and playing well with others and was turned out of office in 1977 after only one term.

An example was Davis' last-minute opposition to a water-sewer bond referendum. "This infuriated Belk, Burkhalter and the rest of council," the former council member said.

Former Mayor Knox snorted that Davis was Belk's only opposition on council.

Davis, when interviewed for this book, conceded that Belk "did a lot of good for Charlotte. My only argument was that when he wanted something done, he could be a little dictatorial." Davis recalled that during one budget process he suspected that Belk and other council members had a secret meeting and worked out an arrangement whereby Belk would abruptly and "illegally adjourn the (regular budget) meeting to prevent me from speaking." In a newspaper report of the meeting, Chafin was quoted as saying, "I'm not surprised (that they left). You embarrassed them, Lou, and I think they were afraid you'd do it again." She was referring to Davis' stand on the water-sewer bond issue.

"Later, at a televised meeting, he (Belk) cut me off and said I had already made those points. And when Harvey (Gantt) and I think it was Neil (Williams) and Betty (Chafin) defended me, Belk walked out," Davis said.

Davis said that because Belk and Burkhalter were so close, the playing field wasn't even. Davis said he couldn't get staff cooperation even though the city manager, city attorney and city clerk were supposed to work for the council, not the mayor. Davis noted that the city manager's position is a political one, however, and he has to align himself with where the power is—and there was no doubt that the power lay with Belk.

Davis said that just after Burkhalter was hired, Belk put him up at the mayor's hotel at Myrtle Beach because it was just before the election and Belk didn't want to unnecessarily complicate the election campaign. "So from the beginning, he and John were very close," Davis said. Burkhalter gave a slightly different version. He said he arrived in Charlotte on a Sunday and was prepared to start work the next day. But an administrative assistant called him at his hotel in Charlotte and said to take a tour of the Carolinas and attend a state city managers meeting in Wilmington for the next week—or until the run-off election was over. Otherwise, the administrative assistant quoted Belk as saying, if an incumbent were defeated, Burkhalter might get the blame.

∞

After the 1975 election, Belk was forced to appoint members to three committees. "No one in charge likes committees," Belk's successor Harris said nearly 20 years later. Belk named Pat Locke to be chair of Public Works and Planning, Jim Whittington to head Operations, and Joe Withrow to head Finance.

∞

A move to call a referendum on district representation passed council by a 4-3 vote in October 1976, but Belk surprised everyone by using a virtually unknown and heretofore unused power—the veto of an ordinance that had not received five votes. The power was somewhat limited and was more of a delaying tactic than an actual veto because the action in 1969 by the General Assembly had provided that five votes were sufficient if council brought the matter back up later. And that wasn't all; City Attorney Underhill subsequently said the veto authority applied only to ordinances and the district representation item was a resolution. Nevertheless, Williams and Chafin admitted they were stunned by Belk's action. Belk argued at the time that voters ought to be able to vote for a majority of council—not five of 11 as under the proposed plan. He also suggested that district representatives be required to live within the district they were to represent, but that they be voted on citywide such as in Atlanta at the time. Although support of district representation was seen in some quarters as a "liberal" or "small-letter democratic" position to take, it was also seen in Charlotte as a means to get Republicans elected to council more easily. The result, however, was that fewer payroll-meeting businessmen—or businesswomen— were elected thereafter. Former Mayor Knox said later that district representation didn't turn out as intended, but did help elect more blacks.

Belk's action merely delayed the inevitable. The voters later approved district representation, but by a scant 170 votes. Belk had warned in letters to the editors and other forums that district representation would impede growth of the city, create "horse trading" among council members and mean the district council members would not represent the city at large on some issues. Incidentally, the city had had district representation in 1851–1917 and 1929–45.

Betty Chafin Rash lamented 17 years later that the districting plan she and Gantt had pushed was not adopted. Not only did the council lose the initiative, but she believed a council of five district and four at-large council members would have appealed to a larger segment of the community, she said.

One former council member said that Belk once grew furious over the district representation issue while council members were gathered in a hotel room on an out-of-town convention trip. "It was a tirade," the former council member said, but it was effective and some council members praised Belk for his passion about an issue he cared so deeply about.

Rash said when interviewed for this book that she didn't recall the episode but said Belk "loved playing the host" when the council was at a National League of Cities meeting or a similar function. Belk would organize the dinner, pick out the wine and usually knew the proprietor at restaurants all over the country. Hence, he'd get a big welcome, Rash said. "He was so tall and so gregarious, everyone knew he was the mayor of Charlotte. Later, when I'd go to such meetings, people would come up and ask about Mayor Belk and I'd tell them he was no longer mayor. He was a legend in his own time. He and Pat Hall were both larger than life."

Chapter Eleven

Race Relations—Things Continue to Improve

While saying that race relations topped his predecessor's agenda, Belk added that his method of dealing with racial matters was to work through Fred Alexander, who served on City Council and later in the State Senate.

Belk said his approach was to let Alexander be in the forefront. The former mayor said he and Alexander confided in each other on many occasions. Belk also gave credit to Johnson C. Smith University's students for acting responsibly during the days of racial unrest that rocked the nation.

Former County Commission Chairman Charles M. Lowe years later also spoke of the Belk-Alexander relationship. "He loved Fred and Fred loved him," Lowe said. At Alexander's funeral in 1980, Belk quipped that Alexander "was a man of great patience. He tried my patience many times."

∞

Federal District Court Judge James B. McMillan had

made his ruling in 1969 that local schools were not sufficiently integrated. Belk, Charlotte-Mecklenburg School Board Chairman William E. "Bill" Poe and Lowe sought to get the United States Supreme Court to act on the appeal of McMillan's order and even went to Washington to meet with Justice Department officials to gain support. That failed. The situation was deemed a crisis and Belk said he was prepared to call in the National Guard to preserve order. A desegregation plan was finally approved by the courts and implemented in September 1974. In May 1974 Belk had declined to speak out on the issue, saying that would make him "too nosy" and that schools were funded by the county, not the city. Poe said in 1993 that he recalled only one lengthy conversation with Belk on the issue.

Belk, Poe and Lowe issued a joint statement in February 1970 asking citizens to "refrain from defiance of and disrespect of the court-order (school) desegregation plan." At the same time, Belk said he was against involuntary busing to achieve school desegregation.

Poe recalled nearly a quarter of a century later that he, Belk, Lowe and School Board Attorney Ben Horack flew to Washington to try to convince attorney Charles Rhyne (a Mecklenburg County native and Duke graduate who was close to President Richard Nixon and had been chairman of the American Bar Association) to represent the school board in the desegregation case. They were not successful, however, and on the trip back, the weather turned nasty. Over Danville, Virginia, it was so bad that the pilot had to circle because he could not go any further in the storm. Poe said he recalled Horack quipped, "I can see the headlines tomorrow: 'The mayor, the school board chairman, the county commission chairman and an unidentified lawyer go down in Virginia.'"

On the school desegregation issue, Belk, in his unique way of Belkese, which got across wisdom in the most unusual ways, was quoted at the time as saying:

"I said that there were some towns that did have to have their patrolmen go in and control school rooms. I said this is how much people can get emotionally upset over school situations because of all the species of animals, the deadliest species is the female. And when you start messing with the female and the young, this is where nature takes over.

"Take the elephant. When I was over in Africa, the bull elephant is not too dangerous but the female is. She had the young. The lioness—she's the one that does the killing. The big tom cat, he doesn't do the killing. So, if you get the mothers of all these children emotionally upset because of the schools, this is what I say is the danger and that's the reason I say that is dynamite because it can explode when you do not get the ladies and their children. This is what I was talking about on that and that's the reason I say it is so important.

"I think we will find a solution like we have on everything else although there is that danger. I mean there's nothing that you can, you know, play around with. They talk about Camelot, you know. That was supposed to be a perfect city. It didn't rain until after sundown and by nine o'clock the moon was always shining and the fog was lifted by 8 a.m. And you can just keep on saying they controlled the legal limit of the city. Well, we've got a better city than Camelot. And if we don't do something about our city I think it will go away. This is what I've been talking about."

Belk, however, came in for some harsh criticism from *Observer* reporter Frye Gaillard in Gaillard's book, *The Dream Long Deferred*, because of Belk's not taking a more significant leadership role. One 1974 *Charlotte Observer* cartoon drew Belk as Nero fiddling while the school crisis burned.

After a picture of one Charlotte-Mecklenburg student slapping another appeared on the front page of *The New York Times*, Poe said he, Belk, the police chief, sheriff and others met to discuss the situation. Poe said Belk said that if the schools couldn't take care of the problem, maybe he as mayor ought to exercise emergency powers and take over operation of the schools. "I just said, 'Give us a chance,'" Poe said 20 years later.

One local political leader, who asked not to be identified when interviewed for this book, noted that one of the problems of the school situation was that the leaders were "Poe, a righteous Baptist, and McMillan, a righteous Presbyterian, both of whom were confident they knew the mind of the Lord exceedingly well."

This same person said that Belk's major "moral contribution (in the area of race relations) was keeping his mouth shut" because, while he didn't agree with forced busing, he saw a consensus was building on the other side of the issue as far as what was best for the community. "I prayed and thanked God that he didn't speak out," the person said.

Kat Crosby, an educator involved in all aspects of civic life through the Brookshire and Belk years and beyond, said years later that Belk's contributions were in improving the physical part of the city and enhancing its image. "He was not a pioneer (in racial matters) but he was kind to individual blacks," she added. Belk created opportunities, she said, but not as openly as had Brookshire. Crosby was close to Fred Alexander and agreed with others who said that Alexander and Belk were also close.

Belk said he believed that Poe and McMillan both acted disgracefully as far as the school situation was concerned, and not in the best interests of students. McMillan, Belk said when interviewed for this book, was too concerned with the legalities and not concerned enough with the effect on the students. Poe, who was chairman of the school board from 1966 through 1976, countered that he thought he and the board acted with "grace and honor . . . I don't know what he (Belk) meant." Poe said he believed the school board represented the wishes of the community at large in the positions it took.

McMillan recalled that he had several conversations about the school situation with Belk, who invariably said, "What the hell's wrong with the local schools?" McMillan said he told Belk and others who questioned him about the schools that he (McMillan) had held similar views as they did until he spent month after month researching the issue.

The judge said that Belk "never made an improper request or demand" on the school issue or any other issue. And, he added, "I don't recall an unpleasant conversation with either John (Belk) or Stan (Brookshire)."

McMillan, who was 76 in 1993, said he viewed Brookshire and Belk as "very different, but both good men." He said both were direct in their dealings with him, even though "I saw very little of Stan . . . I don't recall ever having a private conversation with him . . ."

"If John said he'd do something, he would. If he said he wouldn't, he wouldn't . . . John is a very bright guy, a good-hearted guy . . . John's not argumentative. He either goes along with your assumptions or he doesn't. He doesn't fight with you. Stan had a shorter fuse," McMillan said.

Asked if he thought Belk ever supported his (McMillan's) rulings on the school situation, McMillan answered, "I never thought about it that way. I never discussed it (gaining Belk's support) with him. I just talked about the merits of the case," the judge said. The school case, McMillan said, "had a barrel full of fact and a thimble full of law."

McMillan, who was shunned by many old friends because of his school rulings, speculated that Brookshire and Belk drew a lot more criticism from the voters. "People are afraid to talk to a judge." He did recall that he regularly got a call from a man, apparently a third shift factory worker from the noise the judge said he heard in the background, at 2:30 or 2:45 a.m. "He'd say, 'You son-of-a-b——,' and hang up."

Although Belk was known to shake his head in disbelief over some of McMillan's rulings, he nevertheless continued to play golf with the judge even though some of the judge's old friends had begun to shun him.

Years later, Belk said it made no sense to him to get so mad at anyone that he'd not speak to him or her. "I told people I might be wrong. You have an opinion and stand by it, but you're not always right," Belk said in 1993.

∞

It was suggested years later that Belk viewed some with more liberal views than he as "misguided, but their hearts were in the right place." Also, because John Cunningham and Warner Hall, the chairmen of the Community Relations Committee, which often led the charge in racial matters, were Davidson men and Presbyterians, Belk went along because he identified with those backgrounds strongly, even if not always with the views the two men held.

∞

The city was having trouble making the Concentrated Employment Program effective in 1970. The program was designed to find and motivate the hard-core unemployed.

∞

City Manager David Burkhalter in the spring of 1974

complained that the Charlotte Area Fund was paying people to fight City Hall. He said these people came before council claiming they had the support of the taxpayers. But, Burkhalter asked, what about the council members themselves, who had drawn as many as 25,000 votes in elections?

∞

By March 1974, the Model Cities program was five years old and was battling with the Community Relations Committee. Belk complained that the news media gave agitators higher standing than their support within the community deserved.

The Model Cities and Charlotte Area Fund programs overlapped to some extent, but the former had much greater financial resources. Although officials of the two organizations worked together well at times, some tension still existed. Paul Jones, who headed the Model Cities program, and Robert Person, who headed the Charlotte Area Fund, had several meetings in the late 1960s to try to resolve the conflicts. Betty Chafin Rash, then Betty Chafin, worked for the Charlotte Area Fund in two stints in the late 1960s. Her theory, as expressed 25 years later, was that Model Cities produced duplications of the Charlotte Area Fund's work.

Most of the programs of Model Cities and the Charlotte Area Fund were spun off and some existed under the aegis of city government in 1993. The Charlotte Area Fund, which even ran the Head Start Program in its first few years, had a budget of $5 million in 1970–71, but it had dwindled to $400,000 by 1977. Early on, it was highly controversial because its staff organized welfare recipients and public housing residents, but the fund had a much lower profile in later years. Sam Kornegay, who had been with the fund for 12 years and had been its executive director for four and a half years, resigned under pressure in early 1978. The fund was still alive in 1994 although it was reduced to smaller programs such as employment, homeless assistance, income management and weatherization.

UNC Charlotte political scientist Schley Lyons observed when interviewed years later that "there was money in the war on poverty, but the poor didn't get it . . . It was a failed experiment in centralized planning."

Municipal government in the past, under such mayors as Brookshire and Belk, "had concentrated power and once they made up their minds to do something, they could do it. The power structure did do things. Now government (with greater citizen participation) is more complex," he said. "There are competing legitimate demands. Knowing what to do and how to put together coalitions to get it done is difficult," Lyons said.

Lyons added that average citizens became more cynical because, while they didn't like the way such groups as blacks and women were excluded in the past, they didn't like the inertia of today's government at all levels. "We have designed a system that makes it harder for a mayor to accomplish things like Brookshire and Belk did," he said.

∞

In January 1974, a proposed annexation plan was stalled when four black Charlotteans, James Ross, Julius Cousar, Reginald Hawkins and Ezra Moore, said the annexation would dilute the voting privileges of black citizens.

∞

After Fred Alexander was elected to the State Senate, it was generally agreed that City Council should name a black person to succeed him and several names were mentioned. The vote came December 17, 1974, and architect Harvey

Gantt was proposed. The three Democratic council members voted for Gantt, but the three Republican members voted against him. Belk broke the tie and Gantt was on council. Gantt was to become a force on council and subsequently was elected mayor. The GOP had wanted James K. Polk and later grumbled at the method of selection—saying that citizens had no say-so and that Polk's name was never even formally introduced.

∞

Early in 1975, Gantt brought up the proposed anti-discrimination ordinance then before the local legislative delegation—only to have Belk rule him out of order. But Belk said it was only a procedural action and that he favored the ordinance, which gave the Community Relations Committee power to arbitrate complaints in the areas of housing, employment and public accommodations. The county commissioners opposed the proposal.

∞

Charlotte got its first black assistant city manager, Wylie Williams, during Belk's and Burkhalter's time at City Hall. Williams, who spoke fluent Spanish, was Belk's interpreter on a trip to Charlotte's sister city to Arequipa, Peru.

∞

Warner Hall, who had succeeded John Cunningham as chairman of the Community Relations Committee, stepped down in early 1977 and was replaced by radio-newspaper executive Sis Kaplan.

∞

Charlotte inaugurated its scattered site housing program in February 1975 with no more than 50 public housing units to be at each site. One of the first projects was the Addison Apartments on East Morehead Street.

Pat Hall, a longtime close political ally of Belk, was chairman of the Charlotte Housing Authority in 1976. Under his leadership Charlotte really got going on scattered site public housing. A former top city official said years later that at first blush Belk and Hall were not the most logical candidates to bring about such a progressive development, but upon greater consideration, they might have been the only leaders to have accomplished it. Belk said that had Judge McMillan had his way, every block in the city would have a representative percentage of blacks living there. "We'd have had the same kind of problems in real estate that we had in the schools . . . We thought scattered site housing was the best way to handle it and he (McMillan) went along." The authority's annual report that year said nearly 12,000 residents were in 3,758 units.

Former School Board Chairman Poe said nearly 20 years later that he met with City Council members and CHA members during this period to see if the scattered site housing program might be an alternative to busing students across town.

∞

The Southern Regional Council issued a report in February 1976 charging that Charlotte might have used federal revenue sharing funds to discriminate against women and minorities. Belk labeled the charges "ridiculous" and "untrue."

∞

Plans for a statue of Dr. Martin Luther King Jr. in Marshall Park were in the works in early 1977.

∞

City Council said it would go to court rather than accept black job quotas for fire and building inspection departments as proposed by the Equal Employment Opportunity Commission in answer to charges of discrimination. Councilman Jim Whittington, sitting in for an absent Belk, cast the tie-breaking vote. The next step was formal proceedings against the city by EEOC. The matter was eventually resolved in the late 1970s, City Attorney Henry Underhill recalled later.

∞

No one saw Belk as a leader in the civil rights field as Brookshire had been. Yet he was not perceived as a barrier to the progress unleashed under his predecessor. And whatever his private views on racial matters might have been, publicly his comments were conciliatory and not racist.

Chapter Twelve

The Downtown Is Transformed . . .
and Becomes the Uptown

Charlotte got $3.2 million in Model Cities implemen-
tation funds in 1969, but Paul Jones resigned as executive
director of the program in mid-1970 after having been
accused of being high strung and dictatorial. Assistant City
Manager Carstarphen took over on an interim basis and
helped restore public confidence in the program. Preston
D. Wiley was named as acting director until a permanent
replacement could be hired. Even though Jones had been
under fire, Carstarphen said the resignation came as a
surprise. But when Jones offered it just before a City
Council meeting was to start, City Manager Veeder accepted it immediately. Carstarphen said that while Jones
had his problems, he was popular in some segments of the
black community because of the high position he had
achieved in city government. The consensus seemed to be
that Jones was a good promoter and poor administrator.
Kat Crosby, an educator who was involved in all aspects of
community life from the Brookshire years through the Belk

years and into the 1990s, said that Jones was a good salesman, but it would have been better to pick a local person who understood Charlotte.

But the Model Cities program also was hampered by the shift of emphasis on social issues from the Johnson to the Nixon administration. Former Mayor Belk said nearly a quarter century later that he considered Jones a disaster and guilty of stirring up unrest rather than easing tensions. Jones ended up in the Nixon administration. James S. Wilson took over the job in December 1970 and was in charge until the summer of 1972 when David A. Travland became the first white director of the program.

The program had begun to click in mid-1971, yet Carstarphen had to defend it in a newspaper story written by Mike Dembeck of *The Charlotte News* in April 1972. Dembeck's story questioned whether the $9.2 million in federal funds really had had any impact. Carstarphen admitted that the impact on crime, housing and education was not as great as he had hoped, but he went on to argue that the residents in the Model Cities area were better off than before, even if the program was slow in getting going.

On one occasion Mecklenburg County Commission Chairman (later United States Representative and still later North Carolina Governor) Jim Martin, asked, "Do you really think it's worth it (speaking of the Model Cities program)?" When Carstarphen answered in the affirmative, Martin replied, "Well, you are one of the few who still believe in it!"

"Model Cities was a pipeline of gold from Washington," said Bill Guerrant, who headed the city's public service and information department through most of Belk's period in office. "The intentions were good, but what was done was not based on what people needed but with the attitude: 'Here's what you need.'" As an example, Guerrant said in 1993 that a lot of pocket parks were created but not in the right places with the right equipment and later were not properly maintained. Another example was the rehabilitation of homes, which was fine, except the residents were not taught the skills to take care of their rehabilitated homes and thus, after two or three years, the homes were back the way they originally were. "The people had not bought into it," he said. The citizen input, although so much more extensive than in the past, was still not at the level that the people thought they really had a sufficient voice. "Therefore, the programs had no staying power," Guerrant said. Some of the programs were taken over by existing city and county departments and some just died out when the money dried up during the Nixon administration.

Crosby said that Model Cities did empower some people and she specifically mentioned one woman who was trained under the program, later received a master's degree and was making a contribution as a trainer in 1993. But, Crosby said, the overall impact was minimal.

∞

In January 1970, Belk named lawyer Robert Lassiter, who a year before had been the odds-on favorite to be mayor, as head of the committee to get the $10.7 million civic center (later renamed the Convention Center) constructed on a tract of land offered by the Southern Railway and worth $1 million. The $10.7 million was approved in an overall $36.1 million bond issue passed in December 1969. Money was also there for air conditioning the city's coliseum on Independence Boulevard, street improvements, parks and other uses. Belk put all his energies, enthusiasm and power behind it. He said he was heading the Bond

Squad. The most controversial item in the nine-part bond issue was for the civic center. Insurance man and sometime-politician Jim McDuffie headed the opposition effort.

The plan to have the Charlotte Development Association, made up of private investors, build the facility had been dropped because of legal tangles and the problem of getting approval from the North Carolina General Assembly. The association still planned a $50 million investment in the 25-acres around the center. But it now appeared the College-Brevard-Second-Third streets location would not be suitable for financial and technical reasons.

Belk, two decades later, was critical of Southern Railway for its role in the situation. "They've been a poor citizen," he observed.

The civic center's new proposed site was bounded by Trade, College, Fourth, and the railroad tracks, where the city controlled the land. Belk said in 1993 that a civic center would never have been viable at the location originally proposed because no hotel would be there to support it. The Convention Boulevard proposal, first suggested in 1966, had by then been dropped because of lack of funds in 1969 over the objections of banker Jack Tate. Tate had led the committee charged with pushing the Downtown Master Plan and had run for mayor against Brookshire. Tate felt the incumbent wasn't sufficiently committed to pushing downtown revitalization. Banker George Broadrick headed the drive to convince voters to support bonds for the civic center. He later was miffed because he had argued his case on the grounds that it would be built at Brevard and Second streets so when it was moved, he felt betrayed. Belk in 1993 said that Broadrick was a "highly ethical, straight-laced Christian and felt it was dishonest." But the situation had changed and the city did what it had to do, Belk said.

Assistant City Manager Carstarphen explained at the time that the shift was essential to revitalize the downtown area. The new site was closer to the city's core, Carstarphen said. In addition, the elevators and ramps necessary for the Brevard site would add to the cost of the facility. Lassiter stayed with the project until November 1971 when the civic center was under construction. Once finished in September 1973, Belk suggested it looked like "the Egyptian pyramids." Belk said that President Gerald Ford noted that the Civic Center was called "a white elephant," which suited him, as a Republican, fine.

Belk said the next step after the civic center was to get an office building. Wachovia was approached but Scott Cramer of that bank had become disillusioned about Trade Street and wasn't interested in building at Trade and Tryon. Belk then approached NCNB and convinced its leaders to build on the city's land.

Then came the search for a hotel developer. No one would consider it but Radisson, which did have the "wisdom" to build its hotel on the site, Belk said. So then the civic center-office building-hotel package was complete.

Belk observed what many others said then and later— he had contacts across the nation to put the package together—probably better than any man who ever sat in the mayor's chair before and after. Those in the know agreed that Belk's role cannot be overemphasized in this key development in the downtown area.

William E. "Bill" Poe, former chairman of the Charlotte-Mecklenburg Board of Education, later praised Belk's vision in seeing that the downtown or uptown area could be rebuilt and the drive to make it happen.

"My neck was stuck out, but I had to get something out of the ground," Belk noted years later. Brookshire's major emphasis had been on race relations and while he laid the groundwork for the revitalization of the downtown area—and he honestly believed it to be high on his priority list—others thought much more needed to be done. Evidence of this was Tate's decision to run against Brookshire in 1967. On the other hand, Belk also faced some sentiment in certain circles that too much emphasis was placed on downtown development.

The irony is, Belk said when interviewed for this book, that the new Convention Center was going on the site originally proposed more than 20 years before.

Stan Kaplan, active in communications and politics here over the years, said when interviewed for this book, that downtown/uptown Charlotte could not have been revitalized without Belk—because of his power—but his power within the community, not because he was mayor. "He pushed the town ahead in an orderly way. He sucked up his gut and sold land. He deserves to have an expressway named for him . . . He gives a damn about this town . . . When it comes to a tie vote, he'll vote for Charlotte."

Sis Kaplan, Stan's wife, who likewise has been very involved in political, civic and business circles in Charlotte for years, also praised Belk and noted that officials with similar power in other cities sometimes hurt their cities more than helped them.

The Civic Center did not do as well as hoped for the first few months. Former Mayor Brookshire blamed the Charlotte Development Association for not coming through with the $50 million in development promised. That group admitted it had moved slower than expected, but blamed the lack of liquor-by-the-drink and other factors for the delays. At that point, only the $5.7 million Carolina Trade Mart and the $2.3 million NCNB Corporate Services

Center had been built. But the consensus then and in 1994 was that the NCNB development at the Square, the Jefferson First Union Tower and the Southern National Bank building had been spurred by the center. Burkhalter said the block of land on which the NCNB and Radisson Hotel development stood brought in only $56,000 in taxes to the city and county the last year before the new project came into being.

∞

Small businessmen along East Trade Street displaced by urban renewal took the city to federal court and even charged Belk with conflict of interest because he held NCNB stock. NCNB had acquired the land for its project at the southeast corner of Trade and Tryon. The tenants refused to move so Belk let one furniture store move into a building he owned across College Street.

Many within city government and also among the business community were irked by the court cases brought by the small merchants. The suits cost the city considerable money and one former city official branded the actions as a form of "blackmail." Construction of the Civic Center was held up in April 1971 amidst charges by city officials that each month's delay would add $50,000 to the then estimated cost of $10.7 million.

∞

Former Mayor Ken Harris said a major coup of Belk's administration was getting Addison Reese to move his NCNB headquarters across Tryon to the corner of Trade and Tryon. He praised Belk for working to improve uptown in spite of the criticism he received and the suspicion that the mayor was doing it to enhance his own store on North Tryon. Harris said he believes Belk's motives were pure, "but it took someone with clout to get it done."

At one point, Belk had said that had he wanted to practice conflict of interest, he would have located a civic center at SouthPark, where he had major holdings and which opened in 1970.

∞

More than $6 million in bonds approved in 1969 had improved College, Second, Third and Fourth streets as well as streets in the Model Cities area. The $23 million in bonds approved in 1973 went to extend Tyvola from South Boulevard to I-77, for the Kings Drive relocation, the Randolph Road widening, the Trade-Fourth connector, the Caldwell-Brevard connector and the widening of Poplar.

∞

A half-million dollars for pedestrian bridges over East Fourth, South College and East Trade was approved in May 1975 and they were in use by 1977. Critics said the pedestrian walkway across East Fourth would substantially help Belk's downtown retail store. The walkways had been proposed before Belk became mayor and opened in February 1977. Belk's successor Ken Harris recalled in 1993 that the idea for pedestrian walkways came from a visit of city leaders to Minneapolis.

∞

In 1970 Belk predicted Charlotte would outstrip Atlanta in percentage growth in the 1970s and in early 1972 he was pushing the importance of planning for the future. He called it a very crucial time in the life of the city, particularly in terms of annexation and downtown growth. The start of the NCNB complex was seen as the major item on the downtown agenda.

∞

The "Blue Heaven" Park, which had been touted but

never built, seemed doomed in July 1969. One site suggested was where the Adam's Mark stood in 1994. Eventually, however, Marshall Park graced the city where ugly slums had once been located.

∞

Demolition was started in March 1971 to clear land for a downtown library park. It was finished and dedicated by Belk the following November. The library was extensively remodeled 20 years later.

∞

Belk named Reece Overcash, then president of American Credit Corporation, to head the drive for passage of a $53.8 million bond package in the fall of 1972. Unfortunately, 10 (including money for streets, urban redevelopment and other needs) of 13 items failed. The voters did vote $28.5 million in bonds for the airport and water and sewer facilities. The $28.5 million was the largest bond passage approved by the voters to that date. The losing portion of the bond package was restructured and offered again the following April when $23 million was approved for streets and expressways. Belk was credited with passage through his aggressive campaigning and showing "contagious sincerity." To be sure, Charlotte had as mayor a highly enthusiastic cheerleader who also knew how to accomplish things.

∞

The U.S. Department of Housing and Urban Development rejected plans to redevelop Third Ward in January 1973. The city's Urban Redevelopment Commission, first established in late 1957, had been replaced by a community development department within city government in June 1973 following the phasing out of federal urban renewal programs by President Nixon. Vernon Sawyer remained in charge of the function. Demolition of First Ward dwellings was held up by Federal District Court Judge McMillan in December 1975 on the issue of the adequacy of replacement housing. Belk was still waiting for a lifting of the ban as he left office in 1977. First Ward was bounded by East Fifth, the Brookshire Expressway, Brevard and the Seaboard Coast Line tracks.

∞

Charlotte Observer reporter Marion Ellis wrote a long feature story on what was said to be the city's worst slum— the area bounded by Tryon, Mint, Independence Boulevard and Summit—in October 1973 and then came back to do another analysis piece in early 1975. Lack of money still was preventing meaningful improvements, Ellis reported.

∞

At one time or another McMillan held up I-277, the development of the NCNB building, development of the airport, the Wendover leg of the belt road and urban redevelopment. Just before he was appointed to the bench in 1968, he told a news reporter that, "You will have to judge in time whether I am a judicial activist or traditionalist. Perhaps neither label fits." The judge handled 31 cases filed against the city at one time or another, Belk said years later. But the city eventually got all the projects back on track. McMillan's involvement with City Hall wasn't limited to construction projects and environmental impact. He ruled in December 1971 that the city couldn't legally fire a worker in the building inspection department just because he was the grand dragon of the North Carolina Ku Klux Klan.

∞

Belk said that he really didn't understand why McMillan did what he did, "but Claudia (Belk's wife) understood him and I guess she understood me. So when we were at some function together, she'd sit between the judge and me . . . McMillan was very honest and I thought he was sincere. But I think he hated to make decisions and hoped someone would make them for him."

∞

By the fall of 1974 merchant Jack Wood apparently had won his long battle to get the central business district called "uptown" rather than "downtown." Wood, former proprietor of Jack Wood Ltd., argued that he was not giving the inner city a new name, just reviving an old name. When he was growing up, he said he and his friends would roller skate to the Square (Trade and Tryon). "The fact was you had to roller skate uphill to get there," he recalled. The real fun, he added, was coasting back home down Trade Street. Therefore, everyone in his youth called it "uptown."

The issue arose again in early 1993, when architect David Wagner, chairman of the communications committee of the Charlotte Chamber of Commerce's Central Charlotte Division, asked for citizen input. In a column in *The Charlotte Observer*, Wagner said that a major signage program was under way and that, with the construction of the new Convention Center and the possibility of an NFL stadium, the issue was important. So, he asked for an opinion of whether it should be uptown, downtown, center city or whatever. Nothing new had happened by early 1994.

∞

In August 1975, President Ford's administration made the first of the Community Development Block grants to Charlotte—$10.6 million.

∞

The First Union Tower was finished in 1971 and was the tallest building in the Carolinas. The Civic Center opened in 1973, the 40-story NCNB tower in 1974 and the Radisson Plaza was under construction. Pedestrian walk-ways—or overstreet malls—were still in the works. The Radisson Plaza Hotel was opened in February 1977.

Sue Myrick, Charlotte's mayor in 1987–91, said when interviewed for this book that she also believes Belk's greatest legacy is rebuilding the uptown area. Although he sometimes was accused of working in his own self interest, Myrick said he was unselfishly working for Charlotte's good.

∞

A $16.6 million bond issue was sent to the voters in April 1977 to provide funds for Discovery Place, Spirit Square and water-sewer lines ($16.5 million water-sewer bonds had been rejected six months before) and to allow annexation of 29,250 persons in outlying areas. Belk had opposed the annexation a year before. The voters also were asked to vote on district representation. All measures passed.

∞

U.S. News & World Report reported in 1976 that $185 million had been invested in Charlotte's central city since 1970.

The same story quoted Harvey Gantt, then a member of the City Council, as saying, "We don't have a white noose around the neck of the central city that's happened in a lot of Northern cities and large urban areas. People who move in to take advantage of the city also have to pay their fair share of the costs."

∞

Charlotte became the nation's 50th largest city in mid-1977.

∞

Between 1963 and 1975, 11,115 housing units were

demolished by urban renewal, highways and code enforcement. Belk said that while almost 30,000 people were relocated, "we got few complaints."

But Charlotte's Public Information Director Guerrant said in 1993 that the "sparkle (of urban renewal) was tarnished because of the huge clearance programs. The people saw Earle Village and said, 'Is this what we want?'"

Educator Kat Crosby said urban renewal was a big mistake as it related to the black community. The thrust was "let's renew downtown Charlotte at any cost," she said, "and they removed a whole page of history."

Second Ward, with all its churches, businesses, theaters and the YWCA, was gone—and residents were relocated into "substandard, cheap places." Blacks were given "just enough money to think they had something," she said, but were pushed out on West Boulevard. Black people didn't see Second Ward as slums, she said, but whites decided they were. "We don't make decisions, we make comments," she said in 1993. The best solution would have been to give Second Ward residents enough money to upgrade their properties and allow them to keep their land. "It was so sad," she said. "They didn't tear up white neighborhoods. You never heard of them herding white folks out of their neighborhoods."

McMillan blocked the First Ward urban renewal project between 1975 and 1977 on the issue of relocation, but when the city revised its plans, the judge lifted the ban and let the project get back on track.

∞

Fourth Ward redevelopment was under way in 1977 under the leadership of Dennis Rash, who was then at UNC Charlotte but later headed NCNB's (NationsBank) Community Development Corporation. Rash had been quoted in the April 5, 1976, issue of *U.S. News & World Report* as saying:

"When I moved here 10 years ago, it seemed to me Charlotte desired more than anything else to be a 'junior Atlanta.' What seemed to be the panacea for life and vibrance in the inner city was a strong convention trade."

Rash went on to say he saw a change by 1976 as local banks developed a unique financing plan to begin renovation of the 28-acre Fourth Ward, then 50 percent vacant and deteriorating with 600 residents. Rash predicted 8,500 would live there by 1986. Rash reported 17 years later that the population prediction fell short—because the tax laws were changed—but about 4,000 did live in Fourth Ward. In addition, he said, the assessed tax value leaped from $6 million in 1975 to $90 million in the next 20 years.

∞

Projects completed between 1971 and 1979 downtown included the NCNB Plaza, $35 million; Southern National Center and garage, $30 million; First Union Plaza and garage, $25 million; Wachovia Center, $20 million; Radisson Plaza Hotel, $18 million; Carolina Trade Mart, $9 million; and Northwestern Bank Building, $6.5 million. But much of retailing had fled the uptown area and Trade Street was a hang-out for prostitutes. Ironically, Belk, the businessman, was to close his uptown store in 1988, further eroding the area as a retail shopping center. The store, which had opened back in 1895, was to give way to the $300 million NationsBank–Performing Arts Complex. "He's not an uptown player anymore," one Charlotte leader commented later. "He pushed unpopular things like the Civic Center even when he was accused of doing it to help his store," the person, who asked not to be identified, said. "But I think he did it to help the city." Betty Chafin

Rash, who served on the City Council during Belk's last term, said she sees one of Belk's major accomplishments as revitalizing the uptown area, so it is an irony that he moved his store out of the central city, thereby "killing retail" there. Ironically, only a few weeks after she made the statement for this book, the Belks announced in March 1993 that they were returning to uptown Charlotte with a small Belk Express store in the NationsBank Plaza shops on the Square.

Mayor John M. Belk

Claudia, Mary Claudia and John Belk at the dedication of I–277 as the John Belk Freeway April 5, 1982. Then current Mayor Eddie Knox is holding the umbrella. Governor Jim Hunt is on Belk's left.

Mayor John Belk and Councilman Fred Alexander at a 1975 bridge dedication. City Manager David Burkhalter is the starter. Humpy Wheeler appears over Alexander's shoulder.

Bill Veeder and Mayor Belk at Veeder's retirement ceremony.

Top: *Sandra Townsend, president of the Charlotte Board of Realtors; Walter O. Hendrix, president of the Home Builders Association of Charlotte; County Commission Chair Liz Hair; and Mayor Belk in 1977.*

Above: *Claudia Belk and Mary Claudia in December 1973 just after Mayor Belk's election to his third term in office.*

Bottom: *Claudia Belk and Mayor Belk at campaign headquarters just after the 1975 election victory.* Charlotte Observer reporter Jerry Shinn is in the background.

Former Mayor Belk and Dr. Billy Graham at Graham's 60th birthday celebration November 4, 1978.

Mayor Belk and City Manager David Burkhalter.

Key staff members during the Belk years—Front row: *Bill Guerrant, Cara Mullis, Paulette Purgason, Vi Alexander, Ann Marsh, Carol Jennings, Belinda Crowell.* Back row: *Bill Stuart, Paul Bobo, David Burkhalter, Belk.*

Former Mayor Belk during an interview on Bill Friday's North Carolina People television program.

Reunion of the Belk Administration—Milton Short, Josh Birmingham, Robert Hopson, Herman Hoose, Jake Goodman, Ruth Armstrong, Belk, Jim Whittington, Belinda Crowell, Jack Fennell, Lee Dukes, David Burkhalter, Joe Withrow, Bill Veeder.

Pat Hall and David Burkhalter in a television interview.

Mayor Belk's 1973–74 City Council—Ken Harris, Jim Whittington, Belk, Milton Short, Joe Withrow, Pat Locke, Neil Williams and Harvey Gantt.

Chapter Thirteen

Roads—A Never-Ending Problem

The John Belk Freeway (Interstate 277) was dedicated in April 1982. The Northwest Freeway had been renamed for former Mayor Stan Brookshire in the fall of 1975.

Belk worked hard to get I-277 built, former City Traffic Engineer Herman Hoose later recalled. Belk also was a major promoter of I-77, Hoose said. Former City Manager David Burkhalter recalled in 1993 that he, Hoose and Belk went to Raleigh in October 1971 to campaign for I-277 and were assured by state highway officials Lauch Faircloth and Billy Rose that the contract would be let immediately. But, Burkhalter added, it wasn't until 10 years later that the freeway was finally completed and dedicated.

∞

Federal money was held up for six years by Federal District Court Judge James McMillan because of the ramp near Charlottetown Mall (in 1994 Midtown Square). The ramp took a portion of what had been used as an athletic practice field for Second Ward School, by then gone, but plans ran into federal environmental impact regulations.

∞

Betty Chafin Rash, who served as a member of council during Belk's last term, said she remembers his picking her up at UNC Charlotte, where she was then associate dean of students, so they could have a chance to discuss the transit workers strike. As they were driving along the Brookshire Freeway, Rash said she asked Belk what the city should name for him (Belk). Belk looked astonished, she recalled, and answered, "Nothing, I have all those stores (the Belk stores) named for me."

∞

Belk attended the April 1970 ribbon cutting of the section of Harris Boulevard between U.S. 49 and Mallard Creek Road, which was essential to University Research Park. He was also part of a delegation to visit New York City in March 1972 to help lure IBM to the research park.

∞

Traffic related capital bonds were defeated by the voters in September 1972, but passed the following April as Belk campaigned hard and successfully for the $23 million bond issue for streets and expressways.

∞

Hoose recalled that Belk was a major supporter of road programs. Belk often went with Hoose to Washington and Raleigh to gain support. And although Hoose said he and City Manager Burkhalter were friends and remained so after they left City Hall, Burkhalter was not as much a supporter of roads and highways as his predecessor Bill Veeder had been.

∞

Probably no other department head was as feisty and independent as Hoose. "I always figured I could get (another) job," he said years later. At times, Hoose said, he would implement a project and then inform council members about it. Hoose said some projects, such as the Charlottetown Mall, ended up encroaching on city rights-of-way. Hoose said he wasn't about to insist that the buildings be torn down—he simply arranged for a land swap.

Hoose lamented in 1993 that not enough new streets were being built. He said public transit works only on grid streets with high density. Charlotte has neither, he said.

Hoose continued his push for downtown parking restrictions through Belk's tenure, just as he had during his predecessor's terms. In 1972 Third and Fourth streets were converted to the one-way status they still were in 1994.

∞

McMillan briefly blocked the widening of Sharon Lane between Providence and Sharon roads in March 1972 due to lawsuits filed by attorney Hugh Casey. Halted at the same time was construction of I-77 between Oaklawn and I-85 until the city adopted additional environmental measures.

∞

Car pools were proposed in November 1973 with some vague sort of controls also suggested. Response over the first seven months was far short of expectations—only 1,000 signed up out of a goal of 20,000.

∞

In mid-1975 Belk complained that the city's number one problem was federal red tape and noted that no federal starts on highway projects had occurred for 13 months because of an environmental ruling.

∞

The belt road controversy erupted again in September 1975 when residents of Wendover Road charged the road was no longer needed. Construction on that link had been held up by court action on the part of the Wendover residents. Belk contended that it wasn't fair to have built the Eastway and Woodlawn links and not the Wendover section. The anti-group charged that the Wendover loop would enhance Belk's SouthPark holdings and that Belk was covering up some of the engineering facts, but the mayor emphatically denied this. In February 1976 state and city experts told City Council that studies justified the $6 million, 4.6-mile section of the belt between Eastway and Woodlawn. Don Reid (later a member of City Council) of the Neighborhood Action Committee asked Governor James Holshouser to intervene because Reid contended that the belt was being completed to serve SouthPark.

On July 2, 1976, City Council gave the green light to the section and said the Wendover portion should be 44 feet wide, not 48 feet as engineers proposed, in order to preserve Wendover's water oaks. But the belt road issue stayed before McMillan a few months longer. He declined petitions to halt work in November 1976.

∞

The infamous orange Brookshire barrels were still in use as Belk's terms came to an end. The Brookshire Freeway had been proposed when Brookshire was in office and the barrels were designed, according to Bernie Corbett, then director of traffic engineering, "to protect motorists from one another." They were a source of irritation to motorists and a source of humor for drive-time radio personalities.

∞

The closing of Sherwood Avenue at Queens Road in 1977 resulted in Belk being bombarded with letters from irate neighbors and citizens across the city. The barrier was removed, but not before a major controversy erupted.

∞

Belk and Burkhalter were attacked in April 1974 for

moving too slowly on handling transit matters. Time and federal dollars had been lost, the news media said.

∞

A mass transit center and parking garage was suggested for East Trade, Brevard, East Fourth and the railroad tracks in September 1974.

∞

The voters were asked in April 1975 to approve $2.5 million to buy the transit system and to approve paying for operating losses out of the property tax. The voters agreed to allow the purchase of the transit system from private owners, but said no to paying for operating losses, then running at about $42,000 a month. That left City Council in a quandary as to how to run the system. The vote on purchase of the bus system was 16,426 to 15,089 and the vote on the tax levy for operating the system was 11,667 to 18,978. The system was acquired in 1976.

∞

The voters also rejected a $500,000 item for bikeways, but okayed $1.5 million for 32 miles of sidewalks. In October, Belk broke a council tie to allow the request for bids for a less expensive bikeway between West Charlotte High School and Eastway Junior High School.

∞

A strike by transit workers was narrowly averted in October 1970, but a 36-day transit strike did occur in late 1976—the first such strike since the 26-day strike in 1958. City Coach Lines was then operating the system and uptown merchants complained that the strike had a disastrous effect on their businesses. About a year after Belk left office, his successor Ken Harris had to deal with a 54-day strike, which again seriously cut into uptown business.

Chapter Fourteen

Airport Development—Entering the Big Time

Douglas Municipal Airport in 1969—and 1977—was still much more like a convenience store than the impressive facility of the 1990s. One could see, hear and be heard from one end of the terminal to the other.

∞

But why was the new terminal put where it was? "Cause that's where the planes land," Mayor Belk said. That logic was not unlike another Belkism: "This would solve the solution."

∞

Ross Knight was airport manager when Belk took office, but died in 1970 and was replaced by Edwin Petro, who served less than a year and was then succeeded by R.C. "Josh" Birmingham, who held the job until 1988. Birmingham had been assistant director of public works.

∞

Airline boardings continued to climb—to 814,598 in 1970, 836,382 in 1971 and then topped one million in

1972. Leonard C. Campagna was designated symbolically as the one millionth passenger in December 1972. He got on an Eastern flight to Orlando and received a plaque from Belk because of the distinction. The final total for 1972 was 1,041,000 and in 1976, Belk's final full year in office, the total was 1.34 million.

In late 1977, just after Belk left office, Charlotte-Mecklenburg School Board attorney William Sturges was designated as the millionth passenger to board a single airline during a single year and was recognized ceremonially. Sturges and his wife were on an Eastern flight to New York City.

∞

Belk opened the new north concourse in November 1969. The ribbon cutting for the $200,000 west concourse came in December 1971.

∞

Voters approved $6.25 million in airport bonds in September 1972 as part of a total $28.5 million bond package (the rest going for water and sewer needs).

∞

After two years of wrangling, Yellow Cab got permission to start limousine service from the airport to downtown Charlotte in early 1973. The service started the following September with a charge of $2 for a one-way trip.

∞

Airport expansion of $126.7 million was proposed in September 1974. Included was a new terminal a mile northwest of the old terminal, to be ready by 1980. It was predicted that air traffic would increase from 1.1 million boardings in 1973 to 2.5 million in 1980 to 6.7 million in 1995.

Birmingham had been saying since 1973 that Charlotte

must have a new terminal by 1980, but *The Charlotte Observer* and other critics, specifically in the Steele Creek community, countered in 1975 that the recession had greatly reduced the level of airline traffic and a terminal would not be needed until 1982 or even 1985.

Voters rejected the proposal to sell $55 million in bonds for airport expansion, including a new terminal, in a $92 million bond referendum put to them in April 1975. The $55 million would have drawn an additional $40 million in federal funds, thereby building the new terminal.

∞

The city planned to extend Woodlawn from where it then ended at South Tryon and I-77 to I-85, serving the airport. The bond issue was set up so that the bonds were of the general obligation variety, backed by the tax base, rather than revenue bonds, because of the lower rate of interest and because the city wanted to control airport development, not share it with the airlines. Despite this, the intention was to pay the bonds off from airport revenues.

The voters weren't buying and rejected the airport bonds, as well as money for bikeways and operating the transit system.

The 1975 defeat was a casualty of a battle for control of the black community. The Black Political Caucus had been formed to break the lock Fred Alexander, a former city councilman and later state senator, had on black voters. Bob Davis, president of the caucus, said after the referendum votes were counted that he was "tired and elated" and that it showed "people are more important than things." Harvey Gantt, who had been named to City Council to replace Alexander a few months before and was later to serve as mayor, was behind the bonds. The city's voters generally fell into three groups—Southeast Charlotte, black voters and

Northeast. Two of the three groups were needed to win virtually any election. The Black Caucus picked the airport bonds, which Alexander backed, as a test case—and won by helping to defeat the bonds.

Charlotte businessman Don Davidson, who later was to head the Charlotte Chamber of Commerce, headed the bond campaign and blamed the defeat on the state of the economy. Asked the day after the vote what the city would do in the wake of the loss of the airport and bus operation issues, Belk said candidly, "I haven't the slightest idea."

The vote on the airport bonds was 16,888 against them and 14,575 for them. Funds for airport expansion were approved in June 1978 after Belk left office.

∞

The $21.6 million 10,000-foot runway was under construction at the time. Federal District Court Judge James McMillan in late summer of 1975 halted construction for three years after a lawsuit was filed by the Steele Creek Community Association objecting to the noise that would be created. McMillan held up paving the runway, pending revision of the environmental impact statement.

Years later in 1993, the focus of the judge's memory was much more on his school decisions rather than on the various other decisions affecting city government. Despite support from the Chamber of Commerce and others for resumption of work, work was still halted in June 1976.

The new 325,000-square-foot terminal opened in 1982, at which time the airport's name was changed from the Douglas Municipal Airport to the Charlotte/Douglas International Airport. (The terminal included a million square feet by 1992.)

∞

Belk and Burkhalter, in a *Charlotte News* interview in

March 1975, said that the importance of Charlotte's airport was similar to that of the railroad 100 years before.

∞

The airport suffered some negative publicity in late 1975 when *Newsweek* magazine cited Douglas Municipal Airport as one of the five worst airports in the nation. Four fatal crashes had occurred during the year. And Eastern Airlines Flight 212 had crashed in September 1974 with 72 casualties.

∞

The first scheduled international air cargo flight began in 1978 with the Flying Tigers' route to Zurich, just after Belk left office.

∞

Betty Chafin Rash, who served on Belk's last council, said she recalls nominating Ralph Easterling from the westside to serve on the Airport Advisory Committee. Just after, she said she was at the Festival in the Park and heading for the stage to be recognized when Belk, Veeder and Luther Hodges Jr., then Chamber of Commerce chairman, cornered her and said such an appointment would destroy airport development. She didn't back down, although recalled in 1993 being intimidated by being surrounded by three tall men. She said she firmly believed the appointment turned out to be a good one.

∞

Ken Harris, who succeeded Belk in the mayor's office in 1977, said in 1993 that Belk noted to him that he had not achieved what he wanted as far as the airport was concerned. Harris, a pilot and a 20-year veteran of the Air National Guard, shared Belk's determination to develop a major airport. He said Belk challenged him to get the bond money to proceed to build the terminal. Voters did approve

$47 million in airport bonds for the terminal in mid-1978 during Harris' term and the terminal was opened during Mayor Knox's tenure in office.

Former Mayor Harvey Gantt said he considers Belk's determination to make sure Charlotte got a great airport as his greatest monument. And some said Belk was miffed when Gantt didn't find a way to keep Belk on the Airport Advisory Committee after his legal time expired.

Bill Guerrant, who served as head of the public service and information department during most of Belk's tenure, agreed that the airport was probably Belk's greatest legacy, even if much of the work was finished after he left office. Belk knew, Guerrant said in 1993 when he still headed the public information area, that if Charlotte did not develop a major airport complex, some other city in the area would. Belk's stature in Raleigh and Washington was such that he could accomplish things another man in the mayor's chair couldn't have, Guerrant said. "A lot of what was done in the 1980s and 1990s was planned in the 1970s (under Belk)," Guerrant said. And, he added, Belk continued to serve the cause of the airport after he left City Hall, and was named to the Airport Advisory Committee.

Bill Lee, chairman of the board and president of Duke Power Company when interviewed in 1993, said he considered Charlotte's airport one of Belk's greatest legacies. "For the past 25 years, John Belk has been a driving force in bringing the airport to where it is," Lee said. The "multiplication of that one resource has been enormous. I talk to prospects who are considering moving here and what helps Charlotte compete is its transportation (facilities)." Lee said other cities simply don't have the "quality or quantity" of air transportation to compete with Charlotte. Belk's "relentless pursuit" of continuous improvements was a major key behind the airport's development, he added.

As with other issues, Belk "was impatient with problems caused by the courts," Lee said. "But he persevered."

∞

Belk noted years later that the public thinks of the airport primarily in terms of the terminal, but that more money had been put into the runways and other airport developments than the impressive-looking terminal.

Chapter Fifteen

Planning and Parks and Related Things

A tree ordinance was before City Council in 1977, near the end of Mayor Belk's tenure in office. The ordinance was eventually passed when Ken Harris was mayor and gave the city far-reaching powers despite the fact that it was very brief and concise.

∞

As first proposed in 1968 by Councilman Jerry Tuttle, the city asked for $7 million to build a canal—shades of Venice—on Sugar Creek. Two locations were mentioned—between the Elizabeth neighborhood and Princeton Avenue, or between an area near Central Piedmont Community College, under what was then the Charlottetown Mall (later Midtown Square) and on to Freedom Park. Proponents, including Mayor Belk, envisioned shops, restaurants and hotels being built along the canal. Others predicted only a very narrow two-and-a-half-mile park. But Tuttle lost in the 1971 election and the idea died soon after, only to be resurrected briefly in the fall of 1972 and again a year later. The price tag was $11.4 million in 1974, but it still wasn't getting anywhere. In February 1974, city officials thought the canal might stimulate housing development along its path. With no federal funds, the idea was finally abandoned, even though Jim McDuffie used the matter as a campaign issue against Belk in the 1975 election. A walking-jogging path eventually was constructed between Freedom Park and Morehead Street.

City Council in 1975 reallocated $2.1 million set aside for the canal to take care of flooding problems across the city. Flooding had been caused by rapid growth and addition of paved areas. UNC Charlotte professor James W. Clay offered several suggestions to control flooding during a Urban Studies Institute symposium in 1976. He suggested that the city could stop taxing areas hit hard by flooding, could pay the deductible portions when repairs covered by insurance were made, could buy properties severely damaged, could pay flooding insurance premiums, or could enact ordinances to spread the problem around so other areas would experience minor flooding and relieve flooding elsewhere.

∞

By late 1975, many were questioning the value of the two-year-old Dimensions for Charlotte-Mecklenburg program, which had not drawn as widespread citizen participation as some hoped despite being led by banker C.C. Cameron and former Mayor Brookshire. The program was initiated in 1973 by the Chamber of Commerce, designated as part of the bicentennial activities and funded by the city, county and business. It was patterned after the Goals for Dallas program.

Dimensions was designed to develop—through widespread citizen participation—goals and plans for action leading to an improvement in the overall life of the community in the following 10–20 years. It may have lasted too long—three years, Jane Miles, senior associate director of the UNC Charlotte Urban Institute, said when interviewed in 1993. Some stories in the media at the time questioned whether or not the results were worth the effort. Miles, who was involved in the project, said she believed the participation that did occur justified the program's existence. Citizens were involved and had a forum to air their views and this had value. More than 100 goals were developed and the final report in 1976 could point to progress on several fronts. Whether or not developments that came later—such as the recommended creation of the 911 emergency number—would have resulted without Dimensions can't be determined, she said. Colonel Moe Ward, who directed the program, estimated in 1993 that one-third of the goals had been accomplished.

In his 1975 book, *The Border South States*, Neal Peirce took note of the Dimensions program, but Peirce cited only one goal coming out of the program: "We must maintain an integrated system of education."

∞

Belk dedicated the five-acre Marshall Park and the 124-acre Park Road Park in the summer of 1973. Marshall Park had been named for Charlotte's city manager just prior to World War II. Marshall Park was developed on land that contained the city's most unsightly slums when Belk's predecessor came into office. Park Road Park was located in an area that Charlotte residents considered not suburbia, but the boondocks in the 1960s.

∞

Belk was unable to preside over either the end of the controversial Parks and Recreation Commission, which came just after he left office, or the merger of city and county parks, which came in the 1990s. Residents had grumbled for years about the unresponsiveness of the independent Parks and Recreation Commission—for example, the failure to build a walkway around Freedom Park lake. But it wasn't until parks officials were convinced more money would be forthcoming if they could be funded directly through the city budget that the 50-year-old commission was abolished and replaced with a city department in early 1978. A few steps had been taken back in 1969 when Assistant City Manager Bill Carstarphen got the parks commission to give up some of its autonomy in exchange for greater city support.

∞

In March 1974, Belk and three council members voted against a proposal to change existing multi-family zoning on 360 Myers Park tracts to single family. Although the mayor took a lot of heat from voters and the news media for his stand, the vote was meaningless in a sense because the city ordinances required six council votes to make a change. The City-County Planning Commission in mid-1976 recommended the rezoning to preserve trees, lawns and old houses. Myers Park residents were divided on the issue.

In April 1976, council finally approved the rezoning of 276 parcels in a compromise that generally satisfied those seeking to preserve the status of Myers Park. Belk complained during the five-hour hearing that the council heard from "everyone but Johnny Carson." The winners gave Betty Chafin (later Rash) the major credit for their victory.

∞

The Charlotte Chamber, Central Charlotte Association, and Charlotte Merchants Association pushed for a visitors bureau in late 1975.

∞

After years of controversy, the City-County Planning Commission in June 1977 recommended a small shopping center across Morrison Boulevard from SouthPark—over protests of neighbors. SouthPark itself had opened in 1970. Belk had drawn fire in 1972 when Sharon Lane was widened, thereby making it easier for customers to get to SouthPark, critics said.

∞

Councilman (and later Mayor) Harvey Gantt bought, sold and rebought a tract in Fourth Ward. He had sold the land after finding out elected officials were forbidden by state law to own land in urban renewal areas. But the North Carolina General Assembly later passed a law allowing a primary residence to be purchased.

∞

Belk warned that "Charlotte is behind on its future." And "You can't be unreasonable about something until you get all the facts." And "That is not deductive to good planning." Belk supported good planning and made sure the city looked further ahead in making its plans than had been the situation in the past. "Zoning is one of the most important things whether we are right or wrong," he said.

∞

The Battle of Mecklenburg was reenacted at the Charlotte Motor Speedway in May 1976.

∞

Charlotte's population was 201,564 in 1960, 214,828 in 1963, 226,856 in 1965, 234,140 in 1968 and 241,178 in 1970, as Belk took office. The city's physical size at that point was 73 square miles. The total population for 1972 was 248,400 and 305,000 in 1976. When Belk left office in 1977, the population was 320,000 in 124 square miles.

The city annexed 32.5 square miles and 48,838 people—equivalent to the state's 11th largest city—in 1974. This increased the geographic size of Charlotte by 42 percent and increased the population by 18 percent. Another 29,218 people and 18.4 square miles were annexed in 1977. State law allowed the city to annex urbanized areas without a vote of the people, a provision envied around the nation, particularly in such places as Atlanta.

Belk throughout his tenure stressed beauty as well as growth and said the city had planted 20,000 trees and the county had 13 million trees.

Chapter Sixteen

Making City Hall Businesslike . . .
Strikes . . . and Secrecy

By 1973, Mayor Belk could point to having implemented training for department heads and top supervisors
through the American Management Association and to
having instituted a comprehensive data processing system
to keep up with delivery of services, planning and engineering programs and use of city funds. Charlotte was the
nation's first city to send its department heads through the
AMA programs.

The police department was also involved and the AMA
training did much to upgrade the department's operations,
former Police Attorney Pat Hunter said years later.

Belk had become aware of the AMA programs well before he entered politics. Realizing that neither his Davidson
education nor his military experiences had prepared him
for running the vast Belk retail store empire, he studied
management by attending seminars of the AMA and the
National Retail Merchants Association. He also extended
the national contacts that would help him once he became

mayor by meeting upcoming business leaders such as Ross Perot, who had left IBM and was looking for ways to market computers.

Belk also had insisted that department heads tell him what they planned to do with budget funds allocated— not just say how much they wanted. Budget decisions were not made on a line-item basis as in the past.

Following his first budget process soon after he became city manager in 1971, Burkhalter said he didn't ever want to go through that again. So with the support of Belk and what Burkhalter called "a very competent supporting staff," the city manager instituted the management by objective system and thereby Charlotte became one of the first cities in the nation to do so. The council the next year got a 40-page document to consider rather than one with 400 pages. It said in simple English what the city government planned to do and how it planned to do it and at what cost, Burkhalter said. It took five years to perfect the system and eight years to eliminate all references to line items, he said.

Burkhalter said that he told council members that if he wanted to, he could easily hide something in 400 pages of budget material, but couldn't in 40 pages. Burkhalter said the city also took major steps toward sticking with plans that were adopted rather than abandoning them.

∞

Soon after Burkhalter joined the City Hall team in 1971, Belk instituted monthly breakfasts with top city and county officials as well as Chamber of Commerce leaders in attendance. Usually the meetings were held at the chamber, but when NCNB's Luther Hodges Jr. was chairman of the chamber, the meetings were held in the NCNB Building.

Belk also invited top businessmen and city officials to

a joint meeting at Myrtle Beach and women leaders to a similar session at Lake Norman. By informing the city's business establishment of what was going on at City Hall, it was easier to get their support for various projects.

"Our cities are where the action is and we need more business ability in our civic affairs," Belk was quoted as saying at one juncture. "The city government has lacked management. We are dealing with 2,800 employees and they've got to understand the problems and how to solve them. The better management you have the better organization you'll have."

He went on to illustrate his point with a story about a group of laborers who were ordered to dig holes. They'd dig a hole, cover it up and dig another, over and over. Finally, frustrated with the repetitiveness, they quit. They told the foreman of their decision. The foreman then explained to them that they were supposed to be looking for gas leaks and thus the reason for all the digging. "Now that they understood, it was a different thing, digging all those holes . . . That's management," Belk said.

Belk's homespun approach did not totally disguise his determination to spread efficiency and businesslike practices throughout city government.

∞

Belk also successfully attained more support for the city from its longtime GOP Congressman, Charles R. Jonas of Lincolnton, a firm conservative who opposed virtually all of the Great Society programs. Belk said later he attempted to explain why the city wanted to do what it did and this resulted in a much more positive relationship between Jonas and the city than had existed when Brookshire and his predecessors were mayor.

∞

Banker Graeme Keith was named in the fall of 1969 to push for the local sales tax to be increased a fifth cent, but the issue was defeated in November.

∞

Sanitation workers struck five times between August 1968 and September 1970. The strikes in August 1968, February 1969, July-August 1969 and February 1970 were brief. City Manager Veeder fired 11 workers, who later turned out to be union leaders, in February 1970 when they refused to go out in 13-degree temperatures. Strikers also demanded that Sanitation Department Superintendent Pressly Beaver be replaced in both the February and September 1970 strikes. A strike had been threatened earlier in the summer of 1970, but union leaders tried to prevent it because of the lack of strike funds. At the urging of Belk in September 1970, the city fired 411 strikers, but later hired them back during the strike that lasted almost two weeks. The situation deteriorated to the point that police guards were sent out with the garbage trucks as the city attempted to restore service.

Police Major Sam Harkey was the commander of the police assigned to make sure the garbage trucks that went out were not interfered with, Veeder recalled years later. "He did a superb job. He saw to it that the trucks had no difficulty and at the same time saw to it that the rights of the strikers were protected. His fairness to all concerned probably played a significant role in solving the issue. He was respected by the men working and the strikers alike. Sam Harkey was a first class field commander," Veeder said.

Veeder also recalled that a "young, good looking and articulate" union organizer sent here by the American Association of State, County and Municipal Employees got into an argument with a city employee. The employee picked up a chair and clobbered the organizer and this caused the "organizer to go in one direction and his toupee to go in another," Veeder said. Until then, the employees did not know he wore a toupee and the incident left his credibility weakened. He soon left town, Veeder recalled years later.

WBTV reporter Mike Cozza recalled that television reporters discovered council members discussing strategy regarding the strike at the Barringer Hotel. "They really scampered for the back door when they saw us come in with the cameras," Cozza recalled.

∞

Several of Veeder's key department heads and staffers were told by the city manager to pace themselves during one of the garbage strikes because they'd need to stay alert and full of energy for some time. But, one of them said years later, they stopped off late one night at a Providence Road jazz club for a few drinks and then a few more. When they arrived at City Hall the next morning, somewhat bleary-eyed, Veeder chewed them out unmercifully. It was a vivid memory more than 30 years later!

∞

Also during one of the sanitation strikes, Veeder and Assistant City Manager Carstarphen had been summoned back to Charlotte by Belk from a meeting in California of the International City Managers Association. Veeder was slated to be elected the association's president but missed out when he had to leave. Belk expressed regret for this years later, but defended his decision to recall Veeder because of the importance of his city manager to the city in times of crisis.

∞

A strike by firemen was averted in the summer of 1969.

∞

A top city staffer recalled in 1993 that Veeder was considered anti-union when first hired, but later told other city officials that times were changing and that they needed to accept the fact that some city employees would be unionized.

∞

Rolfe Neill had been a reporter before Stan Brookshire was mayor and came back to Charlotte in 1975 as publisher of *The Charlotte Observer*, a position he still held when interviewed for this book. Soon after he returned to the city, he got Belk and then *Charlotte Observer* Executive Editor David Lawrence, who was also a newcomer to Charlotte, together. "Show us what we ought to see," Neill said to Belk. The mayor took the two newsmen to the waterworks on Belhaven Boulevard. "He wanted to show us we had enough water for a long time to come," Neill said.

Neill added that Belk had a detailed knowledge of the city's operations and also "reveled in getting to know all its employees."

∞

Belk never wanted to be surprised, former State Representative Pat Hunter, who served 10 years as police attorney, recalled years later. Of all the mayors Hunter served with, Belk was the most effective in keeping on top of things, he said. Virtually every Friday, Belk and Burkhalter would go by the police station to be briefed. Hunter said Belk wanted the briefings to be in person and to be concise. "Once, when I was rambling, he said to me, 'You're swimming, but hurry and get back to the bank,'" Hunter said.

∞

Belk was criticized in the media for holding secret meetings. He claimed in mid-1970 that the City Council had violated no laws because the meetings were not secret, just "behind closed doors" or "private."

∞

Belk was a product of a family-owned business and one that conducted its business entirely in private. In his first few years in office, he believed he could get council members together and iron out their differences in a social or private environment—to the benefit of all. Besides, the mayor said, no one had been banned from the meetings. The media countered that if no one other than council members knew of them, they were secret. State law then was somewhat fuzzy on what could and couldn't occur in private. When the new state law was passed, Belk said he believed then and later that he made every attempt possible to adhere to that law. Belk declined to meet privately with council members on several occasions when they suggested it, Burkhalter said years later.

Television reporters were at the center of an episode involving private meetings. A reporter learned that council members were regularly meeting at Belk's home during the weekends with the result that much had been worked out in advance by the time the regular Monday meetings took place. When the reporter arrived at the Belk home, he was let in by the maid and proceeded to film the council members huddled in the den—to their collective dismay.

Bill Arthur, who covered City Hall for *The Charlotte Observer*, took Belk and the council to court in 1971 and charged that the city had violated state law in holding a private meeting December 6 to discuss downtown parking. Reporter Mike Cozza was a key witness because a councilman had revealed to him the subject of the meeting.

Arthur, who had been ousted from the meeting by Belk, filed the suit on behalf of the local chapter of Sigma Delta Chi, the national journalism fraternity. *The Charlotte Observer* itself was not part of the legal action. Ironically, a major fallout of the issue was lowered morale at *The Charlotte Observer* because the paper did not pay Arthur's legal fees, Jack Claiborne wrote in his 1986 history of the paper. Belk and City Council were found in two violations of the state open meetings law in early 1972. These were misdemeanors and the city was enjoined from repeating the practice.

Two other points need to be made.

• *Charlotte Observer* Publisher Rolfe Neill said when interviewed that Belk, who, in addition to being mayor, was the *Observer*'s number one advertiser through his Belk stores, "never, not once sought to get preferential treatment to keep something out or get something in the papers."

Neill said that Belk was surprised at a highly laudatory *Charlotte Observer* editorial that appeared as he went out of office.

• The other point is that *The Charlotte Observer* itself participated in secret meetings with Belk and others at the height of the school busing problems. One newspaper executive admitted that the news was managed at the time, "but with the aim of doing what was perceived was best for the community." Former School Board Chairman William E. "Bill" Poe confirmed the meetings took place. He specifically recalled one that took place at the home of his predecessor, David Harris, with *Charlotte Observer* Editor C.A. "Pete" McKnight and *Observer* reporters present.

Bill Guerrant, who then and two decades later was in charge of the city's public service and information department, said that he is convinced that the secret or private meetings were a factor in the public outcry for district representation in the mid-1970s.

∞

In late 1971, Belk instituted a series of bi-weekly news conferences to counter charges that city government and the public were becoming too distant. Guerrant had been hired in 1970 to help with public information and became director of the public information department the following year. Humpy Wheeler had held the job for a short time before moving on to the American Cyanamid Company, the Ervin Corporation and eventually the Charlotte Motor Speedway. Guerrant recalled that Belk saw that it could no longer be business as usual and city government had to be in closer touch with the people.

In Belk's first term, the city's new department of public service and information handled 7,000 Action Line calls and established the mobile government unit, used primarily in the Model Cities area. Until then, Guerrant said, citizens had no one single number to call. Citizens would scrabble through the telephone book trying to figure out whom to call. Then came information passed on through utility bills.

∞

Belk and Burkhalter made it clear that city government was like a business with many divisions and needed to reflect a cohesive corporate image—to show that the city government's services were all coming from one entity. Until then, many departments had their own logos and own uniforms—and they weren't the same throughout city government. With Belk's merchandising background, he knew things could be done better and that the city "had a good story to tell, but we were not doing it," Guerrant said.

Guerrant said the obvious—Belk was a great cheerleader

for the city. He never hesitated to cut a ribbon or break ground for a new project. And he would climb on a bulldozer or go up in a cherry-picker whenever asked.

∞

Belk believed that the news media sometimes misinterpreted its role and thought it should be advising elected city officials rather than merely reporting the news. He prided himself on always knowing more about what was going on in City Hall than the reporters covering the beat.

Former County Commission Chairman Charles M. Lowe said he believed the news media were "unkind" to Belk. "I don't understand it," Lowe said years later. He said that when he asked reporters about it at the time, they would just shrug and say, "He can take it."

∞

In early 1972, Belk named Mrs. William Hunt to the Charlotte Housing Authority. She was the first female and the first public housing resident to be named to the board. A bi-partisan group of women, including Liz Hair and others, had called on Belk to urge appointment of women to such boards.

∞

Ruth Easterling became the second woman on council in 1972 when the then current council couldn't decide between six men proposed to fill the seat made vacant upon the resignation of banker Pat Calhoun, an NCNB executive. Calhoun faced conflict of interest charges because his bank was involved in development of its headquarters on urban renewal land. Easterling had first been suggested by Claudia Belk, the mayor's wife. Martha Evans, who twice ran for mayor and served in the General Assembly, had been the first woman to serve on the council.

Former *Charlotte Observer* reporter Susan Jetton wrote

then that the selection of Easterling was a perfect example of how the council dealt with issues in the early 1970s. This is how she explained it in a long analysis piece in *The Charlotte Observer*.

After Calhoun resigned, several names were mentioned and such people as State Representative Hugh Campbell and banker W.J. Smith declined to be considered when asked. Alexander had been informed that he had no chance at getting another black councilman selected, so he pushed Dr. Raymond Wheeler, a liberal white. Alexander lined up Councilmen Milton Short and Joe Withrow to vote for Wheeler, giving him three of four votes needed. Although Belk had given indications he might break a tie in favor of Wheeler, that wasn't a sure thing. Councilmen Jim Whittington and Sandy Jordan were adamantly against Wheeler, whom they considered far too liberal. Councilman Jim McDuffie then told Alexander he would support Wheeler so Alexander thought his candidate was a sure thing. Council members were under the threat of a contempt of court citation if they held a closed meeting to discuss the matter, but a lot of one-on-one and telephone conversations took place. Newspaper executive Brodie Griffith's name was put forth. Withrow withdrew his support of Wheeler in the face of pressures and unfounded rumors about Wheeler. Finally, Alexander saw he had virtually no chance to get Wheeler appointed because Belk now gave indications he wanted a unified council decision. So the council vote was unanimous in favor of Easterling. But Alexander and McDuffie were said to have been bitter about the whole episode.

After Jetton's article appeared, Belk quipped, "When did you start writing fiction, Susan?" Withrow and Short were very critical. Whittington surprised her by defending her and saying her story was essentially accurate. Jetton said Short later admitted the same thing—but in private.

As the 1973 election approached, Easterling procrastinated and finally filed for election on her own. But Democratic power brokers pressured her out of the race, hoping to elect Margaret Marrish and thinking Easterling might hurt Marrish's chances. As it turned out, no primary was held, thereby saving the city money. But Marrish lost and the GOP's Pat Locke won to become the city's third female council member.

∞

These were other developments:

• In February 1972, Belk got a letter from his predecessor asking him to a City Club luncheon to hear from "Jim Hunt, the very capable and attractive young attorney who is seeking the office of Lieutenant Governor of North Carolina . . . "

• The Sister Cities program that Brookshire had put so much emphasis on continued under Belk. Sue Myrick, who was Charlotte's mayor in 1987–91, credited Belk's forward vision in what he did with the program. Officials from Arequipa, Peru, visited Charlotte in 1970 and 1971 and Charlotte officials visited that city in 1970. Belk was on hand when Arequipa dedicated its "Charlotte Park" and Arequipa likewise had a delegation here when Arequipa Park was dedicated in front of the main library building at Sixth and Tryon streets. Belk also served on the international Sisters Cities board.

• Belk and David McConnell, general counsel for Belk Stores, were among the financiers of a family movie made in 1973. Called "The Treasure of Jamaica Reef," it starred Stephen Boyd and Roosevelt Grier and was a sunken treasure tale. While wholesome, it didn't even get good reviews in local papers and nothing much was heard of it again. It is, however, listed with two stars out of four possible stars in several television movie guide books.

• Eastland Mall opened July 30, 1975. Belk and County Commission Chair Liz Hair took a turn at ice skating without winning any bids for the Ice Capades. "Mayor Belk and I are used to skating on thin ice," Hair quipped.

• Belk sought having a submarine named for Charlotte in 1976, but it was not until late 1992 that the sub was finally dedicated.

• Claudia Belk drew fire from conservative Baptist corners when she and Gene Owens, then pastor of Myers Park Baptist Church, supported the liquor-by-the-drink forces. The General Assembly finally approved liquor-by-the-drink in September 1978.

∞

Belk asked for a system of a stronger mayor for Charlotte in June 1970. The Institute of Government in Chapel Hill said that Charlotte's mayor had more power than any other in North Carolina, even though that power was limited to voting in cases of ties and a limited veto authority. Belk also suggested that a lobbyist be hired in Raleigh in 1970. The Chamber of Commerce had had attorney Peter A. Gilchrist as its representative in 1969. Attorney Hugh Campbell was the liaison for the city and county in 1975. Then the recently retired U.S. Representative Charles R. Jonas was hired as a liaison in Washington and Raleigh in mid-1974 and was working under City Attorney Henry Underhill. It was made clear he was not to succeed Vince Connerat, the city-county intergovernmental program coordinator.

∞

A city-county consolidation vote was set for March 22,

1971, but much discussion centered on whether the vote should be postponed because of the school crisis and the city election. Belk and a majority of the City Council and County Commission as well as banker C.C. Cameron strongly supported the matter, but School Board Chairman Poe, the small town mayors and lawyer Allen Bailey fought it. The change proposed was that the City Council and County Commission would have been abolished and an 18-member council would have taken their place. In addition, the mayor's powers would have been substantially increased. The vote was an overwhelming "No!"

Councilman Fred Alexander was bitterly disappointed at the defeat and blamed "timid leadership" for the defeat at the polls. Discussion of another vote in 1974 came to naught.

Belk's explanation of the issue in 1974, when he was still pushing the matter, went this way:

"In other words, I see it like this—a monkey never opens a coconut up a tree, he always knocks it on the ground before he gets to the meat. So I think your timing has to be to get the coconut out of the tree to the ground before you decide your form of government . . ."

"Now we've got the coconut, say we'll agree on the time. Say, if they do not agree on the time. They have not agreed now. But say they do."

"Then you have the coconut down out of the tree and they can work on the meat of the coconut, which is the kind of government they would have . . . "

Charlotte Observer reporter Jerry Shinn translated the matter for his readers by saying the coconut stood for consolidation, the meat was the form of government and the monkeys were the City Council members and the County Commissioners.

When asked why some oppose consolidation, Belk replied:

"Well, I guess it's the reason the Lord didn't give a bullfrog wings. He just wants them to bump their fannies as they go along and others fly. Everyone is different, you know . . ."

When a UNC Charlotte survey showed 75 percent responding favored consolidation, the mayor explained that people did agree with the concept of consolidation, but when the specifics were presented, they became opponents.

The 1927 state legislature had approved a bill to allow the city to take over the county if the citizens agreed, but nothing came of it. The matter was studied again in 1949–50. Again nothing.

Former County Commission Chairman Lowe lamented years later that consolidation had not passed, even though he wasn't convinced it would have meant lower taxes. But the voters wouldn't see as much buck passing between the city and county, he said.

UNC Charlotte political scientist professor Schley Lyons quipped to *Charlotte* magazine in 1975 that what Charlotte needed was a good political scandal if any type of real government reform were to be accomplished.

∞

Belk had pushed city-county police merger in 1971 and in September 1975, County Commission Chairman Hair wrote Belk to urge action on the same issue. She then suggested total consolidation in November of the same year. A workshop on city-county consolidation resulted in April 1976. Dr. William J. McCoy of UNC Charlotte subsequently was asked to seek citizen views on the issue, and study district representation and consolidation of park functions.

City and county officials were still discussing the matter in early 1976, but Belk complained that county officials were putting too many conditions on the table—such as a referendum, allowing the county's smaller towns to not be a part of consolidation and including district representation as an essential ingredient.

Already consolidated were the schools, planning commission, tax departments, libraries and utilities.

∞

In January 1970, the issue of public emergency ambulance service came up and it was to come up several other times during subsequent years. Veeder recommended that no changes in the emergency service take place, but added that, if changes were made, the city should handle the service through the police department, not the fire department as the Chamber of Commerce had suggested the previous August. Ed O'Herron, chairman of the Charlotte-Mecklenburg Hospital Authority, rejected Belk's suggestion in the spring of 1974 that the authority take over emergency ambulance service. O'Herron said it would be "unconstitutional." The City Council then proposed that the county take over the system.

∞

In May of 1971 Dr. H. Eugene Peacock of the First United Methodist Church established a committee in response to Belk's challenge about the "soul of the city." Peacock proposed an effort to "lift the level of life for all people" and to propose solutions to moral and ethical problems.

Attorney Allen Bailey in March 1975 called on the council to ban lewd films and obscene publications within the city, but a majority of the council was leery of getting into such a complex issue where enforcement might be extremely difficult. The issue of obscenity had come up several times during the years, usually just before election. City Attorney Henry Underhill warned that an ordinance could be unconstitutional and that the state preempted the city from acting anyway. After a long public hearing, council laid the matter to rest by voting down the proposed ordinance 5-1 (Joe Withrow being the one). The issue came up again in mid-1976 when Pat Locke and Withrow pushed for restricting such materials to special zones. And then in March 1977 council voted to require that covers be put on certain magazines if sold in establishments frequented by minors. The ordinance was amended a month later to allow bare breasts.

Ironically, Judge Claudia Watkins, who later was to become Mrs. John Belk, in May 1969 had found three associates of Ray's News Stand on North Tryon Street, innocent of violating the state obscenity law by selling so-called girlie magazines.

∞

By January 1972 the city manager finally had the authority to hire and fire the police and fire chiefs, an issue long in the discussion stages.

∞

In mid-1974, Belk urged the North Carolina General Assembly to pass the equal rights amendment.

∞

Merger of the water and sewer programs had been on the agenda with little progress for years and years until Belk and County Commission Chairman Pete Peterson got together in the late 1960s to discuss the issue. All sorts of nit-picking issues had raged over the matter for years. Charles M. Lowe, former County Commission chairman, said the Republican-led commission was ready to establish a separate system until Gus Campbell joined the commission and set them straight. When Peterson and Belk met and Peterson tried to bring up some weighty topic, Belk responded, "What about service to Westinghouse?" This happened several times until the two political leaders saw that they were better off getting out of the fray. City staff then worked out a settlement that resulted in the creation of the Charlotte-Mecklenburg Utility Department.

∞

In the early 1970s sports world, Charlotte had the Charlotte Checkers hockey team, two minor league baseball teams (the Hornets and the Twins), and shared the Carolina Cougars basketball team with Greensboro.

∞

A drive in early 1974 to move the American Basketball Association's Carolina Cougars basketball team from Greensboro to Charlotte was backed by Belk, but it didn't happen. Carl Scheer, who later was to reemerge with the Charlotte Hornets NBA organization for a time, was president and general manager of the Cougars. The ABA at the time thought if it could land UCLA's Bill Walton, referred to at the time as the greatest basketball player of all time, the league would succeed. But only 4,000 turned out to see the Cougars play the New York Nets at the old Charlotte Coliseum on Independence Boulevard.

∞

A committee headed by lawyer Dick Thigpen Jr. said in January 1974 that a major sports stadium was needed and economically workable. In April 1974, Belk, banker Hugh McColl, incoming Chamber President Don Bryant, Carowinds owner Pat Hall and others were pushing the need for a 50,000-seat stadium for professional football, but warned it might be as many as six years before one could be built. The estimate was that it would cost $25 million to $50 million, almost equal to the city's operating budget. Airport needs had a higher priority at the time, Belk said. Talk centered first on moving the World Football League's Toronto Northmen or Detroit Wheels here, and the WFL approved the move of the Wheels. Hall considered building a 50,000-seat stadium near his Carowinds facility. But all that happened was that Upton Bell, general manager of the New England Patriots, brought the Charlotte Hornets here for half a season in the fall of 1974 and part of 1975 to play in Memorial Stadium. A game in October between the Hornets and the Memphis Southmen was a success in some respects, but showed the stadium was not geared to handle a capacity crowd. The Hornets lost, by the way, 27-23.

Belk was involved in helping to get financing to keep the Hornets here—and at one point promised to give the team his mayor's salary of $11,000—but insufficient support was found. In September 1975 Belk said that if Charlotte could keep the Hornets alive through 1976, the city would need a 70,000-seat stadium, but the team died. Fred Godley's proposal to enlarge Memorial Stadium from its 24,000-seat capacity to 60,000 by the 1975 season for $6.75 million also died. Then the Chamber of Commerce proposed that a $15-million 50,000-seat stadium be built within the city's inner loop. Belk said the city could have an NFL team here by 1978 *if* the stadium were built. But the mayor said "investments are really sorry right now" and the timing wasn't right to go to the voters to finance it through a bond issue. So Charlotte didn't get its stadium or team.

∞

The gas shortage hit Charlotte in 1974 and long lines were the result. Belk said he was lucky and filled his tank in mid-afternoon, thereby rarely waiting more than 10 minutes. But he urged dealers to find a solution. What was done was an attempt to keep people from topping off their tanks by charging a $3 minimum for large cars and not filling small car tanks until they were at least half empty.

∞

A footnote to the city's 1975 cultural action plan said that the Charlotte Symphony Orchestra and Opera Carolina had outgrown the acoustics of Ovens Auditorium. It would take 17 years for a new home to be ready.

∞

Police Chief J.C. "Jake" Goodman, who had been picked to replace Ingersoll in 1968, was under fire from the Black Solidarity Committee in June 1969 because its members charged Charlotte police were brutally mistreating blacks. Jack Bullard, executive director of the Charlotte-Mecklenburg Community Relations Committee, in October was named to observe the police department's handling of grievances by citizens. Additional police brutality charges were aired in July 1972 and City Manager Burkhalter urged Goodman and Bullard to improve communications between each other and placed a Community Relations staff member on the internal affairs investigating committee when it was involving race relations.

Then in March 1977 Goodman was charged with destruction of unlawful wire taps. He sued *The Charlotte Observer*, which first made the charges public. Ironically, the issue came to light only after an *Observer* reporter went to the home of a policeman on another matter. The policeman didn't answer the door, suspecting the issue was wiretapping. He then went to his lawyer and they made a deal with the federal district attorney. Had the policeman known what the visit by the *Observer* reporter was really about, the wiretapping scandal might never have become public.

Burkhalter said at the time he didn't believe there was any illegal wiretapping or cover-up. But later he said he then believed wiretapping occurred, but that neither Goodman nor his top aides knew about it. It apparently was done by an over-zealous policeman acting individually, Burkhalter said. The controversy went on for four and a half years with council finally issuing a report detailing mishandling of wiretapping by high-ranking police officers. Belk's successor, Ken Harris, had hired GOP lawyer David Sentelle to pursue the matter. Sentelle's report to the City Council included findings that police wiretapping was widespread in the early 1970s. But council recommended no disciplinary action. *The Charlotte Observer* won its libel suit in 1981 after Goodman had retired. Goodman's attorney failed to prove that *The Charlotte Observer*'s actions damaged Goodman, who was never found guilty.

Belk in 1993 still considered Goodman honest and a victim of a vendetta by *Charlotte Observer* Editor Pete McKnight. Belk said that Goodman had contacted McKnight's boss, James L. Knight of the Knight-Ridder newspaper chain, to complain about *The Charlotte Observer*'s coverage of a drug raid. Goodman believed the *Observer* had gone into print on deadline charging police brutality without having the full story. Belk admitted in 1993 that Goodman's contacting Knight may have been ill-advised but that Goodman didn't deserve the subsequent nearly obsessive witch-hunt. The wiretapping charges gave McKnight his chance, "although he couldn't get Jake as long as I was in office," Belk said. Belk said he told Goodman that he would back him as long as he told the truth, but if Goodman lied, Belk would fire him. "It was a personal thing with Pete," Belk said.

Former Police Attorney Pat Hunter credited Belk with "keeping the waters calm" while *The Charlotte Observer* continued its relentless probe and pressured the City Council to suspend Goodman. "He (Belk) was very fair and his support meant a lot to the chief," Hunter said.

∞

Belk and *Charlotte Observer* Executive Editor David Lawrence had lunch together in December 1976 at which time Belk complained that *Observer* staffers didn't care enough about the city Belk led and loved. Lawrence wrote the mayor a lengthy letter arguing that he and his *Observer* staff did indeed care about the city and were committed to making it an even better city.

Belk said years later that he believed the exchange and similar meetings and conversations with television executives helped create a far better understanding of what he was attempting to do at City Hall.

∞

On other police issues, Belk saw that the personal lives of the policemen were in turmoil, so a chaplain was hired to provide advice on their domestic lives. Promotions didn't come without the policemen going through Central Piedmont Community College courses, Belk said, and the result was that some inadequate hold-overs from the post-World War II days were weeded out.

∞

The city also ran into problems, primarily before Judge McMillan again, on such issues as whether the chief had the authority to tell policemen how to cut their hair and where to live. The city wanted to require all members of the force to live within Mecklenburg County. Eventually the city prevailed.

∞

President Ford and his daughter Susan visited the city for the Mecklenburg Bicentennial in May 1975. The celebration commemorating the signing of the Mecklenburg Declaration of Independence included two parades, a historical drama with a cast of 50 (including Mayor and Mrs. Belk as his forefather John McKnitt Alexander and his wife) and a speech by Dr. Billy Graham.

∞

Charlotte celebrated the nation's bicentennial in 1976.

∞

Belk agreed to help Senator Henry Jackson in the 1976 Democratic race for president, but later backed Jimmy Carter's campaign after the former Georgia governor was nominated.

∞

Pat Hall toyed with the idea of running for governor in 1976, but did not make the race and Jim Hunt was subsequently elected. Hall died in 1978 at 56 years of age. Hall had been a major force in the community and was a close friend of Belk. Back in 1967, Hall had been instrumental in putting together the 625 acres needed for the Westinghouse Electric Corporations' $65 million development. And in 1969 he announced a $250-million, 2,000-acre development that would include an amusement park, residential sites, apartments, a convention hotel and a golf course. *Charlotte News* Editor Perry Morgan didn't hold back and called it "the most ambitious undertaking ever announced in Mecklenburg County."

The first phase, the Carowinds amusement park, opened on a rainy day in 1973 on property located on the North Carolina/South Carolina state line. It became a victim of a bad economy and was sold in 1974.

∞

Belk and his wife moved from her old house on Beverly Drive, where they had lived since getting married, to Hempsted Place in mid-1976 to give their daughter, Mary Claudia, who was in college by the early 1990s, more room to play.

Drawing Some Conclusions

To be sure, every Charlotte mayor—certainly every one since World War II—left a mark on the city. But it can be argued compellingly and perhaps convincingly that Stan Brookshire and John Belk had a greater impact than any of their predecessors or successors.

Part of it was the times—they were the right men at the right time. Part of it was that they served longer than any other mayors. Part of it was because they had to share less power than those who followed them in City Hall.

They had their similarities, but also their differences. Both dearly loved their city, although Brookshire's enthusiasm paled in comparison with Belk's because he was more subtle and subdued than the gregarious Belk.

Brookshire, while presiding over changes in such areas as civil rights and urban renewal, did not have to face as many changes not of his own making as did Belk. Belk saw the first Republicans on City Council, as well as being the first mayor to have more than one woman on council at the same time. Belk also had to deal with a more suspicious, prying news media and the rising force of neighborhood groups.

Both faced mostly token opposition except for

Brookshire's last campaign, when John Tate challenged him, and for Belk's first try, when Gibson Smith almost ended Belk's political career before it began. Yet it should be noted that neither Tate nor Smith called for dramatic changes. Major differences on how to run Charlotte were not to come until later.

Both Brookshire and Belk laid solid foundations for a businesslike, efficient way of running City Hall.

There's no doubt that Charlotteans of the 1990s and beyond owe a major debt to the two men who emerged from business to take over the challenges of city government in such a crucial period.

No one can say for certain how Charlotte would have fared had Brookshire not run and instead elected one of his friends such as Ed Burnside, who played a major role in drafting Brookshire, or Martha Evans, who was the early-on favorite to win in 1961. Nor can one say with certainty what Charlotte would have been like in 1994 had Jim Whittington, who coveted the mayor's chair for many years, or Smith or Tate, both of whom nearly did win, succeeded in their quests.

But the city did fare well—better than many of its **neighbors** in the Carolinas and across the South. Thank **you**, Stan and John!

Closing Out the Era

So 1977 seems like the recent past—except for the very young.

Annie Hall was the top movie of the year, *Roots* was the talk of television and no Pulitzer Prize was given for literature.

Eddie Murray was the American League rookie of the year, John Fought was the amateur golfer of the year and Tom Watson won the Masters. Dean Smith's Tar Heels, led by South Mecklenburg High's Walter Davis, were 28-5 and Lee Rose's UNCC basketball team, featuring Cornbread Maxwell, made the Final Four. Walter Payton was the top rusher and Roger Staubach was the top passer in the NFL. George Foster hit 52 home runs, Pelé retired and Earl Campbell won the Heisman Trophy. Bob Quincy wrote in *The Charlotte Observer* that Charlotte's Edison Foard, who had scored the first touchdown in Kenan Stadium, would reunite with his 1927 UNC teammates in the fall. And freshman Famous Amos Lawrence piled up 286 yards as UNC beat Virginia. East Mecklenburg and Charlotte Catholic high schools won state football titles. Lee Fidler and Marjorie Loewer were winners in the first Charlotte Observer Marathon. Frances Crockett's Charlotte O's were the darlings of the minor leagues—at least in terms of promotions. First Union's Lynda Ferreri owned the NASCAR race car driven by Janet Guthrie.

Jim Hunt and James Edwards were paid $45,080 and $39,000 respectively as governors of North Carolina and South Carolina and it cost 13 cents to mail a first-class letter. Isabella Cannon, 73, was elected mayor of Raleigh. Tom Turnipseed announced he would be a candidate for governor of South Carolina in 1978. The Labor Party was replaced in Israel after decades of rule and Maria Callas died.

Spirit Square opened. Jacques Brourman was conductor of the Charlotte Symphony. SouthPark was seven years old and Eastland Mall was two. The Civic Center was renamed the Convention Center.

Our troops were home from Vietnam, but deep emotional scars remained.

Kays Gary was easily the city's best-known and most beloved newsman. A man could get a haircut for $3.50 in Charlotte. Miss Charlotte-Mecklenburg was Kathy Norman, a 23-year-old music teacher and morning manager at Valentino's restaurant. Duke Power customers suffered with power shortages in mid-summer. Betty Feezor, a WBTV personality bravely fighting cancer, was named grand marshal of the Carolinas Carrousel Parade.

Larry Johnson and Alonzo Mourning were just little (?) lads in elementary schools in Texas and Virginia respectively.

Bill Lee was one of two executive vice presidents of Duke Power Company, Hugh McColl was president of NCNB (Luther Hodges resigned as chairman to run unsuccessfully for the U.S. Senate), George Shinn moved his Rutledge Educational Systems headquarters from Raleigh to Charlotte, Jim Martin represented the Ninth District in the U.S. House of Representatives and Johnny Harris lured Equitable Life Assurance Society to Charlotte to be an anchor tenant in The Park, near SouthPark.

Jimmy Carter was still bringing his hometown approach to governing the nation. Jesse Helms and Robert Morgan were North Carolina's senators and Strom Thurmond and Ernest Hollings were serving in the U.S. Senate for the Palmetto state.

Tom Belk was chairman of the board of the Charlotte Chamber of Commerce. Jay Robinson was superintendent of the Charlotte-Mecklenburg Schools. Stan Brookshire was peacefully retired and hardly a force in local politics.

John Belk went back to the Belk department store empire as full-time president. In 1982, five years after leaving City Hall, he was named as Charlotte's most powerful person by *The Charlotte News*. At the time, he was considering running for governor in 1984 and Charlotte lawyer Jim Cole even tried to draft him to run for the GOP. Belk ended up deciding not to make the race, but not before frustrating then-Mayor Eddie Knox, with whom Belk was feuding, and who also wanted to run and get Charlotte money to finance the race. But by 1990, much of the public perceived that the political power Belk once had possessed had eroded. It was suggested by some that Belk simply didn't want the power any more. One person who had followed Belk's career noted that while Belk rarely initiated things anymore, he nevertheless could be counted on to support projects to help the city and still wielded a lot of power behind the scenes. Many new Charlotteans knew Brookshire and Belk only because of the expressways named in their honor and by the Belk department store chain connection.

Former Mayor James Smith was still in Gastonia. Ken Harris was elected Charlotte's first Republican mayor, Eddie Knox was solidifying his position within the local and state Democratic Party and would move into City Hall in two years, Harvey Gantt was on the City Council, Sue Myrick was president of the Myrick Agency, and Richard Vinroot was just out of the Army and beginning to build his law practice.

City Government Officials During the Brookshire and Belk Eras

Mayor and City Council—1961 through 1963

Date Elected	Sworn In	Term
May 2, 1961	May 8, 1961	Two Years

Mayor Stanford R. Brookshire
James B. Whittington (Mayor Pro Tempore)
Claude L. Albea
Don G. Bryant
Steve W. Dellinger
Sandy R. Jordan
Gibson L. Smith
John H. Thrower

City Manager	William J. Veeder
City Clerk	Lillian R. Hoffman
City Attorney	John D. Shaw
	John T. Morrisey—
	Effective August 15, 1961

Mayor and City Council—1963 through 1965

Date Elected	Sworn In	Term
May 7, 1963	May 13, 1963	Two Years

Mayor Stanford R. Brookshire
James B. Whittington (Mayor Pro Tempore)
Claude L. Albea
Don G. Bryant
Steve W. Dellinger
Sandy R. Jordan
Gibson L. Smith
John H. Thrower

City Manager	William J. Veeder
City Clerk	Lillian R. Hoffman
City Attorney	John T. Morrisey

Mayor and City Council—1965 through 1967

Date Elected	Sworn In	Term
May 4, 1965	May 10, 1965	Two Years

Mayor Stanford R. Brookshire
James B. Whittington (Mayor Pro Tempore)
Claude L. Albea
Fred D. Alexander
Sandy R. Jordan
Milton Short
John H. Thrower
Jerry Tuttle

City Manager	William J. Veeder
City Clerk	Lillian R. Hoffman—
	Deceased June 22, 1966
	Ruth Armstrong
City Attorney	John T. Morrisey—
	Resigned August 2, 1965
	James W. Kiser
	Effective March 14, 1966

Mayor and City Council—1967 through 1969

Date Elected	Sworn In	Term
May 5, 1967	May 15, 1967	Two Years

Mayor Stanford R. Brookshire
James B. Whittington (Mayor Pro Tempore)
Sandy R. Jordan
Milton Short
Gibson L. Smith
James B. Stegall Jr.
Jerry Tuttle

City Manager	William J. Veeder
City Clerk	Ruth Armstrong
City Attorney	James W. Kiser

Mayor and City Council—1969 through 1971

Date Elected	Sworn In	Term
May 9, 1969	May 19, 1969	Two Years

Mayor John M. Belk
James B. Whittington (Mayor Pro Tempore)
Fred D. Alexander
Sandy R. Jordan
Milton Short
John H. Thrower
Jerry Tuttle
Joe D. Withrow

City Manager	William J. Veeder
City Clerk	Ruth Armstrong
City Attorney	Henry Underhill

Mayor and City Council—1971 through 1973

Date Elected	Sworn In	Term
May 7, 1971	May 17, 1971	Two Years

Mayor John M. Belk
Fred D. Alexander (Mayor Pro Tempore)
Patrick N. Calhoun   Resigned February 22, 1972
Sandy R. Jordan
James D. McDuffie
Milton Short
James B. Whittington
Joe D. Withrow
Ruth M. Easterling   March 27, 1972
(unexpired term, Calhoun)

City Manager	David A. Burkhalter
City Clerk	Ruth Armstrong
City Attorney	Henry Underhill

Mayor and City Council—1973 through 1975

Date Elected	Sworn In	Term
November 6, 1973	December 1, 1973	Two Years

Mayor John M. Belk
James B. Whittington (Mayor Pro Tempore)
Fred D. Alexander   Resigned November 25, 1974
Pat Locke
Milton Short
Neil C. Williams
Joe D. Withrow
Harvey B. Gantt   January 6, 1975
(unexpired term, Alexander)

City Manager	David A. Burkhalter
City Clerk	Ruth Armstrong
City Attorney	Henry Underhill

Mayor and City Council—1975 through 1977

Date Elected	Sworn In	Term
November 4, 1975	December 15, 1975	Two Years

Mayor John M. Belk
James B. Whittington (Mayor Pro Tempore)
Betty Chafin
Louis M. Davis
Harvey B. Gantt
Pat Locke
Neil C. Williams
Joe D. Withrow

City Manager	David A. Burkhalter
City Clerk	Ruth Armstrong
City Attorney	Henry Underhill

A

Addison Apartments 179
Airport Advisory Committee
   215, 216
Albea, Claude L. 20, 28, 29, 88,
   90–92, 255, 256
Alexander, Fred D. 15, 24, 26–
   27, 36–37, 44–45, 52, 55–
   56, 60, 62, 117, 118, 127,
   130, 131, 133, 137, 150,
   160, 171, 174, 178, 213–
   214, 235, 238, 256, 257,
   258
Alexander, John McKnitt 247
Alexander, Kelly, Sr. 42, 55
Allen, Ivan, Jr. 50–51, 155–156
Amen, Paul 54
Amity Gardens Shopping Center
   41
Anderson, W.L., Jr. 62
Arbuckle, Howard 63
Arequipa, Peru 114–115, 116,
   179, 236
Armstrong, Neil 123
Armstrong, Ruth 256, 257, 258,
   259
Arthur, Bill 231–232
Atkins, J. Murrey 9
Atkinson, Sam T. 118
Atlanta Constitution 128
Atlanta, Georgia 50–51, 53, 77,
   99, 150, 155, 157, 168,
   190, 196, 224

B

Babcock, Randy 26, 28
Bailey, Allen 238, 240
Barnhardt, Mrs. L.E. 109
Barnard, Christiaan 6
Barnhardt, William H. 126
Barringer Community 83
Baxter, Herb 139
Beasley, C.C. 14
Beatty, Jim 133, 148

Beaver, Jeff 1
Beaver, Pressly 228
Beeson, Clarence E. 89, 90, 91
Belk, Claudia 192, 234, 237,
   247. *See also Watkins,
   Claudia*
Belk, John M. 4, 10, 11, 16, 17,
   20, 22, 23, 27, 28, 33, 34,
   44, 46, 57, 74, 78, 80, 82,
   88, 91, 93, 101, 113, 116,
   120, 121, 126–127, 128–
   129, 130–131, 132, 133,
   134, 135, 136–138, 139,
   140–141, 143, 144–158,
   159, 160, 162, 163, 164–
   169, 171, 172, 173–176,
   177, 178, 180, 181, 183,
   184, 185, 186, 187, 188,
   189, 190, 191, 192, 194,
   195, 196, 197, 205, 206,
   207, 208, 209, 211, 212,
   214, 215–217, 219, 220,
   221–222, 223–224, 225–
   226, 227, 228, 229, 230–
   233, 234, 235, 236, 237–
   240, 241, 242, 243, 245–
   246, 247, 248, 249, 250,
   253, 255, 257, 258, 259
Belk, Mary Claudia 134, 153,
   248
Belk Stores 4, 42, 94, 126, 127,
   131, 132–133, 135, 145,
   150, 153, 189, 190, 196,
   197, 206, 225, 232, 236,
   253
Bell, Upton 243
Belmont Community 80
Belton, Moses 52
Belvedere Homes 83
Bernstein, Mark 59, 81
Birmingham, Alabama 50
Birmingham, R.C. "Josh" 100,
   211, 212
Blanda, George 1
Bobo, Paul 22, 160–161

Boger, Mary Snead 15
Boulevard Homes 83
Boyd, Stephen 236
Bridges, Herbert 126
Broadrick, George 92, 186
Brooke, Edward 6
Brooklyn Community 2, 12, 49, 71–76
Brookshire, Edith 57, 116
Brookshire, Stanford, Jr. 12
Brookshire, Stanford R. 3, 7–20, 21–26, 27, 28, 30, 32, 33, 34, 35–37, 38–39, 43–49, 50, 51, 52, 55, 56, 57–58, 59, 60, 61–63, 72, 73–77, 78, 79–82, 83, 84–86, 87–88, 89, 90, 91, 93, 94, 95, 97, 98, 100, 101, 103, 105–106, 107–108, 109, 112, 113, 114–116, 117–119, 120–121, 125, 128, 135, 138, 139, 140, 144, 146, 150, 154–157, 159, 174–176, 178, 181, 183, 186, 187, 188, 205, 208, 220, 227, 230, 236, 249, 250, 253, 255, 256, 257
Brourman, Jacques 252
Brown, Harry G. 75
Brown, Jim 1
Bryant, Don G. 9, 26, 27, 30, 34, 35, 37, 38, 60–61, 72, 73, 85, 89, 91–92, 103, 108, 110, 139, 242, 255, 256
Bullard, Jack 46–47, 60, 63, 162, 244
Burkhalter, David A. 31, 147, 157, 159–160, 161, 162, 163, 165, 166, 167, 176, 177, 179, 189, 205, 206, 208, 214, 226, 230, 231, 233, 244, 245, 258, 259
Burlington, North Carolina 29
Burnside, J. Ed 49, 51, 54, 89, 98, 154, 250

C

Calhoun, Patrick N. 234, 235, 258
Callas, Maria 252
Calley, William 123
Cameron, C.C. 126, 220, 238
Campagna, Leonard C. 212
Campbell, Earl 251
Campbell, Gus 241
Campbell, Hugh 235, 237
Cannon, Carol 143
Cannon, Isabella 252
Carowinds 29, 30, 118, 126, 242, 243, 247
Carstarphen, William H. "Bill" 22, 23–24, 26, 27, 33, 36, 37, 38, 47, 85, 117, 146, 152, 157, 160, 163, 183, 184, 187, 222, 229
Carter, Clyde 42
Carter, James E. "Jimmy" 124, 247, 253
Carter, Mrs. Elisha 89
Casey, Hugh 207
CATV 111
Central Piedmont Community College 113, 219, 246
Centralina Council of Governments 108
Chafin, Betty 138, 165, 166, 168, 177, 222. *See also* *Rash, Betty Chafin*
Chambers, Julius 54–55
Chaplin, Saxby 88
Charles, Donald 35
Charlotte Area Fund 58, 59, 81, 177
Charlotte Chamber of Commerce 3, 7, 9, 21, 30, 45, 49, 50, 51–52, 53, 54, 87, 89, 91, 93, 98, 120, 127, 155, 157, 158, 159, 164, 193, 214, 215, 220, 222, 226, 237,

240, 242, 243, 253

Charlotte Coliseum 53, 79, 158, 185, 242

Charlotte College 5, 113. *See also University of North Carolina at Charlotte*

Charlotte Community Hospital 105, 106. *See also Good Samaritan Hospital*

Charlotte Development Association 84, 186, 188

Charlotte/Douglas International Airport 98, 214. *See also Douglas Municipal Airport*

Charlotte Firefighters Association 35

Charlotte Housing Authority 180, 234

Charlotte-Mecklenburg Board of Education 80, 81, 88, 130, 132, 139, 151, 157, 172, 175, 180, 187, 212, 232, 238

Charlotte-Mecklenburg Community Relations Committee 44, 46, 58, 62–63, 162, 176, 177, 179, 244. *See also Mayor's Committee on Human Relations*

Charlotte-Mecklenburg Government Center 25

Charlotte-Mecklenburg Hospital Authority 106, 240

Charlotte-Mecklenburg Planning Commission 107, 222, 223

Charlotte-Mecklenburg Schools 3, 5, 38, 130, 172, 173, 174, 175, 180, 253

Charlotte-Mecklenburg Utility Department 119, 242

Charlotte Memorial Hospital 105, 106

Charlotte Motor Speedway 2, 223, 233

Charlotte News 2, 9, 14, 17, 33, 53, 88, 90, 103, 105, 110, 127, 128, 184, 214, 247, 253

Charlotte Observer 7, 8, 9, 17, 27, 33, 44, 51, 54, 55, 57, 63, 81, 84, 86, 92, 93, 111, 114, 121, 127, 128, 144, 150, 158, 159, 160, 163, 173, 192, 193, 213, 230, 231, 232, 234, 235, 238, 244, 245, 246, 251

Charlotte Parks and Recreation Commission 3, 108, 221–222

Charlotte Police Department 134

Charlotte Post 52

Charlotte Symphony Orchestra 115, 244, 252

Charlottetown Mall 2, 207, 219. *See also Midtown Square*

Charter Review Commission 107–108

Citizens Advisory Committee on Urban Redevelopment 75

Citizens Bank of Charlotte 75

Civic Center 78, 82, 83, 84, 87, 125, 130, 132, 134, 138, 158, 185, 186, 187, 188, 189, 190, 193, 196, 252. *See also Convention Center*

Claiborne, Jack 232

Claiborne, James "Slug" 52–53, 54

Clark, David 3

Clay, James W. 220

Clemson College 5

Clinton, William J. 30

Cobb, William E. 5

Cole, Jim 253

Collins, LeRoy 45

Committee on City Education 15

Connerat, Vince 237
Convention Center 2, 84–85, 141, 185, 188, 193, 252. *See also Civic Center*
Corbett, Bernie 208
Cormier, Richard 115
Cotswold Mall 2, 97
Cousar, Julius 178
Cozza, Mike 229, 231
Cramer, Scott 62, 187
Crawford, Charles C. 51
Crawford, Earl, Jr. 93
Crockett, Frances 251
Cromartie, Doris 109
Crosby, Kathleen "Kat" 44, 45, 55, 174, 183, 185, 195
Crowell, Belinda 140, 152–153, 161
Cunningham, John R. 42, 43, 45, 52, 176, 179
Curry, Kathleen 128, 129

D

Dalton Village 83
Davidson College 2, 3, 5, 43, 127, 176, 225
Davidson, Don 214
Davidson, North Carolina 20, 133
Davis, Bob 213
Davis, Ernie 1
Davis, Jeff 3
Davis, Louis M. 165–167, 259
Davis, Walter 251
Dellinger, Steve W. 24, 26, 27, 28, 29, 87–88, 89, 90–92, 106, 255, 256
Delta Airlines 98
Dembeck, Mike 184
Democratic Party 10, 17, 22, 136, 254
Denton, Don 120
Dickson, Rush S. 28
Dilworth Community 76

Dimensions for Charlotte-Mecklenburg 220–221
Discovery Place 141, 194
Douglas, Ben E., Sr. 97, 130
Douglas Municipal Airport 97–101, 118, 138, 141, 211–217, 243. *See also Charlotte/Douglas International Airport*
Dowdy, George 94
Duke Endowment 105, 106
Duke Power Company 3, 92, 119, 140, 216, 252
Duke University 1, 5, 7, 9, 24, 50, 172
Durham, North Carolina 43, 131

E

Earle Village 74, 77, 83, 195
East, John 135
Easterling, Ralph 215
Easterling, Ruth M. 234–236, 258
Eastern Airlines 98, 99, 100, 212, 215
Eastland Mall 2, 141, 237, 252
Edmisten, Rufus 18
Edwards, James 252
Edwin Towers 74, 77, 83
Eisenhower, Dwight D. 114
Elizabeth Community 219
Ellis, Marion 192
Englander, Mark 137
Epley, Joe 33, 47, 126, 128, 147
Ervin, Charles 89–90
Ervin, Paul 113
Ervin, Sam 3, 79, 135
Evans, Martha 8, 9, 10, 11, 234, 250
Ezrol, Stanley 137

F

Faircloth, Lauch 205

Fairview Homes 83
Federal Communications
    Commission 112
Feezor, Betty 252
Ferreri, Lynda 252
Fidler, Lee 251
First Union National Bank 85,
    141, 189, 193
First Ward 76, 80, 82, 141, 192,
    195
Foard, Edison 251
Ford, Frederick Douglass 58
Ford, Gerald R. 124, 187, 193,
    247
Ford, Susan 247
Foster, George 251
Fought, John 251
Fourth Ward 56, 76, 80, 195–
    196, 223
Frech, Laura 91
Freedom Park 104, 219, 220,
    222
Friendly Relations Committee
    43. *See also Mayor's
    Committee on Human
    Relations*
Frye, Edward R. 106

G

Gagarin, Yuri 2
Gaillard, Frye 55, 173
Gantt, Harvey B. 3, 5, 20, 46,
    55, 60, 93, 138, 139, 149,
    154, 155, 156, 163, 165,
    166, 168, 178–179, 194,
    213, 216, 223, 254, 258,
    259
Garinger, Elmer 3, 5
Gary, Kays 252
Gastonia, North Carolina 8
Gilchrist, Peter A. 237
Gilmore, Gary 124
Girault, Abel 52
Glenn, John 5

Godley, Fred 243
Golden, Harry 2, 39
Goldwater, Barry 6
Good Samaritan Hospital 104–
    106. *See also Charlotte
    Community Hospital*
Goodman, John C. "Jake" 35,
    36–37, 244–246
Graham, Billy 42, 100, 115, 247
Greensboro, North Carolina 23,
    41, 47, 146, 242
Greenville Community 76, 80,
    82, 84
Grier, Joseph W., Jr. 3, 107
Grier, Roosevelt 236
Griffith, Brodie 126, 150, 235
Guerrant, Bill 31–32, 145, 146,
    147, 148, 161, 162, 184,
    185, 195, 216, 232, 233
Guthrie, Janet 252

H

Hair, Liz 19, 144, 234, 237, 239
Hall, Pat 29, 126, 130, 132, 136,
    139, 154, 169, 180, 242,
    243, 247
Hall, Warner 2, 176, 179
Hammarskjold, Dag 2
Harkey, Sam 228
Harris, David 232
Harris, Johnny 3, 253
Harris, Ken 3, 33, 93, 139, 140,
    154–155, 163, 164, 167,
    189, 190, 209, 215–216,
    219, 245, 254
Harris, W.T. 119, 135, 154
Hawkins, Reginald 41, 42, 44,
    50, 53, 55, 104–106, 178
Haynes, Myles 133
Head Start Program 59, 177
Hearst, Patty 124
Helms, Jesse 81, 148, 253
Henderson, Perrin 129, 130
Hidden Valley Community 62

High Point College 8
High Point, North Carolina 39
Hitch, S. Herbert 9, 28
Hodges, Luther, Jr. 159, 215, 226, 252
Hoffman, Lillian R. 255, 256
Hollings, Ernest 1, 253
Holshouser, James 208
Hood, Dan 81
Hoose, Herman 37, 92–94, 205, 206–207
Horack, Ben 172
Hord, John 36
Horn, Carl, Jr. 92
HUD. *See United States Department of Housing and Urban Development*
Humphrey, Hubert H. 6, 13, 120, 151–152
Hunt, James "Jim" 135, 236, 247, 252
Hunt, Mrs. William 234
Hunter, Pat 225, 230, 246

I

Ingersoll, John E. 36–37, 58, 244
Iowa State University 3
Ivey, George, Jr. 153
Ivey's Department Store. *See J.B. Ivey and Company*

J

J.B. Ivey and Company 42, 76, 153
Jackson, Henry 247
Jackson, Mahalia 42
James, Jesse 28, 29, 35
Jenkins, Jay 114
Jetton, Susan 44, 144, 145, 146, 158, 160, 234–236
Johnson C. Smith University 41–42, 49–50, 52, 54, 59–60, 171
Johnson, Lady Bird 120
Johnson, Larry 3, 252
Johnson, Lyndon B. 6, 13, 45, 79, 80, 114, 184
Johnston, Olin 3
Jonas, Charles R. 3, 12, 14, 15, 79–80, 81, 133, 227, 237
Jones, Charles 41
Jones, Eddie 18
Jones, Mrs. Eddie 18
Jones, Mrs. Edwin 1
Jones, Paul 47, 81, 82, 177, 183–184
Jordan, Everett 3
Jordan, Sandy R. 89, 91, 92, 110, 160, 235, 255, 256, 257, 258

K

Kannapolis, North Carolina 3
Kaplan, Sis 130, 156, 179, 188
Kaplan, Stan 128, 130, 131, 156, 159, 188
Keith, Graeme 228
Kennedy, John F. 3, 5
Kennedy, Robert F. 6, 16, 55, 106
King, Martin Luther, Jr. 5, 6, 44, 53, 54, 59, 60, 104–105, 180
King, Ray 26
Kirkpatrick, Jimmy 56
Kiser, James W. 19, 20, 29, 112–113, 256, 257
Klerlein, Mrs. Edward T. 109
Knight, James L. 245
Knight Publishing Company 76
Knight, Ross 100, 211
Knox, Charles 139
Knox, Eddie 3, 33, 136, 139, 148, 154, 155, 159, 166, 168, 216, 253, 254
Korea 127
Kornegay, Sam 177

L

Lake Norman 2, 119, 227
Larese, York 1
Lassiter, Robert, Jr. 78, 125, 126, 185, 187
Lawing, T.R. 57, 95
Lawrence, David 230, 246
Lawrence, "Famous" Amos 251
Leach, D'Etta 42, 56
Leake, George J. 127, 130, 133
Lee, Harper 1
Lee, William S. "Bill" 3, 119, 216, 217, 252
Lenoir, North Carolina 115
Lima, Peru 115, 116
Lincolnton, North Carolina 133, 227
Little Rock, Arkansas 50
Little, Tom 10
Littlejohn, Frank 35
Locke, Pat 139, 164, 167, 236, 241, 258, 259
Loewer, Marjorie 251
Lowe, Charles M. 23, 113, 140, 148–149, 150, 152, 154, 171, 172, 234, 239, 241
Lumumba, Patrice 1
Lyons, Schley 136, 138, 178, 239

M

Manson, Charles 123
Maris, Roger 1
Marney, Carlyle 2
Marrish, Margaret 236
Marsh, Ann 24, 32, 84, 121
Marshall Park 71, 73, 141, 180, 191, 221
Marshall, Thurgood 6
Martin, Jim 3, 59, 108, 119, 133, 184, 253
Maxwell, Cedric "Cornbread" 251
Mayes, Doug 10, 11, 50, 143,

146
Mayor's Committee on Human Relations 42, 43, 44, 45, 52. *See also Charlotte-Mecklenburg Community Relations Committee*
Mayor's Coordinating Committee 45
McArver, Kenny 2
McColl, Hugh 3, 156, 242, 252
McConnell, David 236
McCoy, William J. 239
McDuffie, James D. 90–92, 133, 134, 135, 136, 139, 186, 220, 235, 258
McGovern, George 123, 148
McGuire, Frank 1
McIntire, William C. 14
McIntyre, William 103–104
McKnight, C.A. "Pete" 51, 92, 232, 245
McMillan, James B. 17, 19, 48, 89, 165, 171, 172, 174–176, 180, 192–193, 195, 205, 207, 208, 214, 246
Mecklenburg County Board of Elections 19
Memorial Stadium 56, 243
Memphis, Tennessee 59, 104
Mercy Hospital 105, 106
Midtown Square 219. *See also Charlottetown Mall*
Miles, Jane 221
Minneapolis, Minnesota 190
Model Cities Program 47, 59, 79, 80, 81, 177, 183, 184, 185, 190, 233
Moe, Doug 1
Moore, Ezra 178
Morgan, Perry 247
Morgan, Robert 135, 253
Morrisey, John T. 24, 30, 33, 37, 73, 107, 112, 114, 117, 255, 256
Mourning, Alonzo 3, 252

Mulliss, William 59
Murray, Eddie 251
Myers, Brevard 28
Myers, Mrs. T.J. 2
Myers Park 1, 88, 89, 90, 222
Myrick, Sue 3, 12, 23, 25, 48, 93, 116, 154, 194, 236, 254
Myrtle Beach, South Carolina 167, 227

N

NAACP (National Association for the Advancement of Colored People) 42, 47, 55
NationsBank 19, 156, 195, 196. *See also North Carolina National Bank*
Neill, Rolfe 148, 163, 230, 232
Neubauer, Herb 137
New Orleans, Louisiana 77, 150
New York, New York 6, 99, 206, 212
New York Times 174
Newton, David 136
Nicklaus, Jack 1
Nixon, Richard M. 6, 82, 120, 123, 124, 172, 184, 185, 191
Nolen, John 87
Norman, Kathy 252
North Carolina Association of County Commissioners 114
North Carolina General Assembly 15, 34, 38, 90, 108, 114, 120, 134, 167, 186, 223, 234, 237, 241
North Carolina House of Representatives 148
North Carolina League of Municipalities 14, 30
North Carolina National Bank (NCNB) 3, 78, 83, 84, 141, 187, 188, 189, 190, 192, 194, 195–196, 226,

234, 252. *See also NationsBank*
North Carolina Senate 44, 137, 171, 178
Northwestern Bank 141, 196

O

Odell, A.G., Jr. 78–79, 83
O'Herron, Ed 240
Ovens Auditorium 55, 158, 244
Overcash, Reece 191
Overstreet Mall 141, 194
Owens, Gene 237

P

Park Road Park 221
Park Road Shopping Center 41
Payton, Walter 251
Peacock, H. Eugene 240
Pearson, Albert T. 13–14, 127, 129, 130, 133
Peirce, Neal 221
Pelé 251
Penninger, Randy 52
Perot, Ross 226
Person, Robert 177
Peterson, Pete 241–242
Petro, Edwin 100, 211
Pfeiffer College 14
Phillips, Craig 5
Phillips, Dwight 10, 54
Piedmont Courts 83
Player, Gary 1
Poe, William E. "Bill" 80, 132, 133, 139, 172, 174–175, 180, 187, 232, 238
Polk, James K. 58, 179
Presbyterian Hospital 105, 106, 134
Purgason, Paulette 161

Q

Quincy, Bob 251
Quinn, Al 99

R

Rafferty, Tom 100, 101
Raleigh, North Carolina 38, 46, 108, 205, 206, 216, 237, 252
Rash, Betty Chafin 18, 32–33, 162, 165, 168, 177, 196–197, 206, 215, 222, 259. *See also Chafin, Betty*
Rash, Dennis 195, 196
Ray, James Earl 105
Ray, Tom 139
Reagan, Ronald W. 120, 130
Reese, Addison 126, 189
Reid, Don 208
Republican Party 136
Rhyne, Charles 172
Robbins, H. Haywood 78
Robinson, Jay 253
Robinson, Joe H. 3
Rose, Billy 205
Rose, Lee 251
Ross, James 57–58, 178
Rouzer, Elmer 3
Rowe, Oliver 10, 82, 126
Rumley, Jim 135
Rusk, Dean 52

S

Salem College 2
Sanford, Terry 1, 49, 59, 76, 100
Sawyer, Vernon 71, 74, 191
Scheer, Carl 242
Scheer, Julian 2
Schwall, Don 1
Second Ward 71, 195, 205
Selvey, Ernest 35
Sentelle, David 245
Shaw, John D. 255
Shinn, George 2, 3, 252
Shinn, Jerry 158, 238
Short, Milton 17, 18, 27, 30, 34, 36, 117, 119, 133, 136, 139, 147, 149, 159, 160, 164, 235, 236, 256, 257, 258
Sister Cities Program 116, 236
Smith, Charlie 18
Smith, Dean 1, 4, 251
Smith, Doug 33
Smith, Gibson L. 14–15, 20, 26, 27, 28, 73, 88, 91–92, 126, 127, 128, 130, 250, 255, 256, 257
Smith, James 3, 8, 10, 28, 43, 75, 98, 126, 254
Smith, W.J. 235
Snepp, Frank 57
Southern National Bank 141, 189, 196
Southern Railway 12, 71, 76, 83, 185
SouthPark Mall 2, 141, 190, 208, 223, 252
Southside Homes 83
Spangler, C.D., Sr. 52, 62
Spartanburg, South Carolina 23
Spaugh, Herbert 151
Spirit Square 141, 194, 252
Staubach, Roger 251
Steele Creek Community 213, 214
Stegall, James B., Jr. 36–37, 257
Stern, Ralph 53
Stith, Pat 33
Strawn Village 76, 83
Strawn, Zeb C. 75
Sturges, William 212
Sweitzer, Charles L. 100

T

Tate, John A. "Jack," Jr. 16–20, 78–79, 186, 188, 250
Tate, Sharon 123
Thatcher, Margaret 153
Thigpen, Dick, Jr. 242
Third Ward 191
Thrower, John H. 21–22, 25, 29–30, 36, 37, 88, 90–92,

110, 157, 160, 255, 256,
257
Thurmond, Strom 3, 253
Travland, David A. 184
Trosch, Minette 154
Tross, Nathaniel 42
Troutman, North Carolina 7
Tucker, Walter 62
Turnipseed, Tom 252
Tuttle, Jerry 118, 160, 219, 256,
257

U

Underhill, Henry 24, 29, 61,
121, 147–148, 161, 163,
167, 181, 237, 241, 257,
258, 259
United Community Services 49,
59
United States Congress 12, 30,
38, 48, 72
United States Department of
Housing and Urban
Development 13, 81, 82,
108, 191
United States House of Representatives 3, 253
United States Senate 3, 252, 253
United States Supreme Court 6,
123, 172
University of North Carolina 1,
3, 50, 113, 251
University of North Carolina at
Charlotte 6, 10, 11, 14, 39,
118, 136, 178, 195, 206,
220, 221, 239, 251. *See
also Charlotte College*
University of North Carolina
Institute of Government 16,
30, 237
University Research Park 119,
206

V

Van Every, Philip 130
Veeder, William J. "Bill" 22, 25,
26, 27, 28–33, 34–35, 36,
47, 58, 60–61, 80, 81, 82,
89, 93, 99, 100, 105, 119,
146, 147, 157, 159–160,
161, 163, 183, 206, 215,
228–230, 240, 255, 256,
257
Vietnam 2, 32, 124
Villa Heights Community 80
Vinroot, Richard 4, 12, 25, 138,
141, 156, 157, 254

W

Wachovia 62, 141, 187, 196
Wagner, David 193
Wake Forest Law School 3
Wake Forest University 54
Walton, Bill 242
Ward, Moe 221
Warner, James R. 137
Washington, D.C. 13, 14, 38,
45, 72, 79, 81, 82, 83, 139,
147, 172, 184, 206, 216,
237
Watkins, Claudia 131, 241. *See
also Belk, Claudia*
Watson, Tom 251
Watters, Pat 52, 53, 54, 77
WBTV 111–112, 128, 229, 252
WCCB-TV 112
WCNC-TV 112
WCTU 112
Wheeler, Humpy 233
Wheeler, Raymond 235
Whittington, James B. 10, 14,
16, 20, 25–26, 27, 28, 29,
37, 90–92, 94, 99, 110,
125, 126, 127, 130, 133,
136, 138, 139, 140, 144,

160, 162, 165, 167, 181,
235, 250, 255, 256, 257,
258, 259
Wiley, Preston D. 183
Wilkins, Roy L. 55
Williams, J.T. 15
Williams, Neil C. 139, 164, 165,
166, 168, 258, 259
Williams, Wylie 179
Wilmer, Henry 134, 137, 139
Wilson, Henry Hall 13
Wilson, James S. 184
Wilson-Bullard Community 83
Winston-Salem, North Carolina
41, 43, 125
Withrow, Joe D. 136, 160, 167,
235, 241, 257, 258, 259
Wood, Jack 193
WRAL 81
WSOC-TV 10, 11, 111–112

X

X, Malcolm 6

Y

Yancey, Henry 10
Yardley, Jonathan 50–51, 155
Ylvisaker, Paul 59
YMCA. *See Young Mens*
Christian Association
Young, Andrew 44
Young Mens Christian Associa-
tion 72
Young Womens Christian
Association 72, 195
Younts, Paul 10, 26, 38, 76, 88,
90, 92, 154
YWCA. *See Young Womens*
Christian Association

Photography Credits

Page 64: Brookshire files

Page 65, top: Belk files
bottom: Photo courtesy of the Robinson-Spangler Carolina Room, Public Library of Charlotte and Mecklenburg County. (Photo by Philip Morgan originally appeared in *The Charlotte Observer.*)

Page 66, top: Brookshire files
bottom: Veeder files

Page 67, top and bottom: Charlotte Community Development Department files

Page 68, top and bottom: Photo courtesy of the Robinson-Spangler Carolina Room, Public Library of Charlotte and Mecklenburg County.

Page 69: Photo courtesy of the Robinson-Spangler Carolina Room, Public Library of Charlotte and Mecklenburg County.

Page 70: Brookshire files

Page 198, top: Belk files (Ken Plott Studios)

bottom: Photo courtesy of the Robinson-Spangler Carolina Room, Public Library of Charlotte and Mecklenburg County.

Page 199, top: Belk files
bottom: Veeder files

Page 200, top: Belk files
bottom, left: Photo courtesy of the Robinson-Spangler Carolina Room, Public Library of Charlotte and Mecklenburg County.
bottom, right: Photo courtesy of the Robinson-Spangler Carolina Room, Public Library of Charlotte and Mecklenburg County. (Photo by John Daughtry originally appeared in *The Charlotte Observer.*)

Page 201: Belk files

Page 202, top and bottom: Burkhalter files

Page 203, top: Belk files
bottom: Burkhalter files

Page 204, top and bottom: Burkhalter files

(continued from front flap)

the Charlotte-Mecklenburg Public Library and *The Charlotte Observer,* and scrapbooks compiled by himself, Brookshire and Belk. He also talked to scores of men and women who were active in the political and business worlds during that period.

There's humor as well as hard facts here. Read how Brookshire avoided an international scandal involving a wealthy Peruvian and a Lenoir, North Carolina, woman. And how British Prime Minister Margaret Thatcher "put down" Belk. Included is information on a heretofore secret meeting held in 1961 with the purpose of finding a way to fire Veeder. New information is also here about how restaurants and hotels desegregated in Charlotte.

*A*lex Coffin, a native of Asheboro and a graduate of the University of North Carolina at Chapel Hill, worked for newspapers in Asheboro; Seoul, Korea; Charlotte; Atlanta; and Vancouver, British Columbia, before joining Duke Power Company's corporate communications department in 1976. He established Coffin Associates/Public Relations in 1985. Coffin also spent two years in Washington as a congressional aide. He is married to the former Sonia Kulka and they have a son, Jonathan Tristram, and a daughter, Anna Sloane.

Photography: Donna Bise

Jacket Design: Barbara Howard

Back Cover: Photo courtesy of the Belk files

UNC Charlotte
Charlotte, North Carolina 28223

$19⁹⁵